To:

From:

Given on:

1.13.24
Ps 37:37

The apostle Paul said in Romans 16:1: "I commend to you our sister, Phoebe, who is a deacon in the church. Welcome her in the Lord as one who is worthy of honor among God's people…she has been helpful to many." I echo Paul's sentiments in regard to Sheila Zellers. I honor her as a great servant of God in the twenty-first century as one who is helpful to many through her ministry.

—Rev. Jesse Owens, President
Global Renewal, Inc.
Bethel, Pennsylvania

Short, practical, bite-size nuggets of wisdom. Until now only available in occasional nibbles but this book holds a whole feast!

—Thomas McCulley, Pastor
New Life Marco
Marco Island, Florida

Sheila Zellers is an anointed woman of God. She has the gift of an evangelist and not only portrays the Word in worship and through her preaching, but demonstrates the Word as a lifestyle. I have known Sheila for thirty years and my wife has known her since birth. We have seen consistency and a life of faithful service to God, her family, and to the body of Christ at large. Sheila is a beautiful display of God's blessings on a life lived in obedience to His calling and committed to fulfilling the Great Commission.

—Keith R. Conley, Senior Pastor
Harvest Assembly of God
Lakeland, Florida

I have known Sheila Zellers since 1989. She has been a true friend to me, my wife, Susan, and our son, Stephen. Sheila has been faithful in her walk of faith and steadfast in her love for God and His holy Word. She is a student of the Bible and a true disciple of Jesus Christ. Sheila is an anointed and gifted preacher, teacher, singer and prayer warrior. It has been said that the two most important days in a Christian's life are the day they were born again and the day they discovered why they were born again. Sheila Zellers has certainly found her calling and her anointing!

—Senior Pastor Grant Thigpen
New Hope Ministries
Naples, Florida

The ways of life have the tendency of causing even the ordinary person to misunderstand the character and nature of God. Sheila continues to bring spiritual, practical, and relevant insight through her unique way of communicating the heart of God towards His children. Each "Selah" prompts the heart of the reader to discover the truths of what God really thinks of them. The Lord spoke to Elijah in 1 Kings 19 and told him that He (God) was not in the wind, not in the earthquake, not in the fire, but the message of God was in a still, small voice. On each page, in each paragraph, within each sentence of *Selahs from God* can be found that whisper of God's agape love speaking to the life, circumstance, faith, and heart of each reader. Be prepared to be swept away by the breathe of God with your daily journey of *Selahs from God*. This book is truly a love letter from the heart of the Father.

—Dr. Randal L. Holdman, Lead Pastor
Parkway Life Church
Naples, Florida

What a great privilege it is to share with you about this exciting new book from Rev. Sheila Zellers. As you read *Selah's from God*, not only will you be moved to go deeper and reach higher for the Father's purpose in your life, but it will allow you to develop a Christlike character and fruit that will remain. It's a must for those who are passionate about kingdom advancement!

—Tony Stewart, Senior Pastor
Citylife Church
Tampa Florida

Selahs
FROM God

Sheila
ZELLERS

**CREATION
HOUSE**

SELAHS FROM GOD
SOMETHING TO THINK ABOUT—REAL LIFE EXPERIENCES WITH
REAL *Word* APPLICATIONS
by Sheila Zellers
Published by Creation House
A Charisma Media Company
600 Rinehart Road
Lake Mary, Florida 32746
www.charismamedia.com

This book or parts thereof may not be reproduced in any form, stored in a retrieval system, or transmitted in any form by any means—electronic, mechanical, photocopy, recording, or otherwise—without prior written permission of the publisher, except as provided by United States of America copyright law.

Unless otherwise noted, all Scripture quotations are from the New King James Version of the Bible. Copyright © 1979, 1980, 1982 by Thomas Nelson, Inc., publishers. Used by permission.

Scripture quotations marked AMP are from the Amplified Bible. Old Testament copyright © 1965, 1987 by the Zondervan Corporation. The Amplified New Testament copyright © 1954, 1958, 1987 by the Lockman Foundation. Used by permission.

Scripture quotations marked ASV are from the American Standard Bible. Copyright © 1960, 1962, 1968, 1971, 1972, 1973, 1975, by the Lockman Foundation. Used by permission.

Scripture quotations marked ESV are from the Holy Bible, English Standard Version, Copyright © 2001 by Crossway Bibles, a division of Good News Publishers. Used by permission.

Scripture quotations marked KJV are from the King James Version of the Bible.

Scripture quotations marked NASU are from the New American Standard Bible—Updated Edition, Copyright © 1960, 1962, 1963, 1968, 1971, 1972, 1973, 1975, 1977, 1995 by The Lockman Foundation. Used by permission. (www.Lockman.org)

Scripture quotations marked NIV are from the Holy Bible, New International Version of the Bible. Copyright © 1973, 1978, 1984, International Bible Society. Used by permission.

Scripture quotations marked NLT are from the Holy Bible, New Living Translation, copyright © 1996, 2004, 2007 by Tyndale House Foundation. Used by permission of Tyndale House Publishers Inc., Carol Stream, Illinois, 60188. All rights reserved.

Note: Some scriptures marked NLT are from the Holy Bible, New Living Translation, copyright © 1996 by Tyndale House Foundation. Used by permission of Tyndale House Publishers Inc., Carol Stream, Illinois, 60188. All rights reserved.

Scripture quotations marked THE MESSAGE are from *The Message: The Bible in Contemporary English*, copyright © 1993, 1994, 1995, 1996, 2000, 2001, 2002. Used by permission of NavPress Publishing Group.

Scripture quotations marked TLB are from The Living Bible. Copyright © 1971. Used by permission of Tyndale House Publishers, Inc., Wheaton, IL 60189. All rights reserved.

Scripture quote of 1 Peter 5:7 in chapter 31, "Cast All Your Cares on Him, Who Is the Burden Bearer" provided by free use courtesy of the Darby Translation, Weymouth New Testament, and the World English Bible.

Design Director: Bill Johnson
Cover design by Nathan Morgan, and Natalie Zellers and Opus Studios

Copyright © 2012 by Sheila Zellers
All rights reserved

Visit the author's website: www.motivatedbylove.org

Library of Congress Cataloging-in-Publication Data: 2011942165
International Standard Book Number: 978-1-61638-748-8
E-book International Standard Book Number: 978-1-61638-749-5

While the author has made every effort to provide accurate telephone numbers and Internet addresses at the time of publication, neither the publisher nor the author assumes any responsibility for errors or for changes that occur after publication.

First edition

12 13 14 15 16 — 9 8 7 6 5 4 3 2 1
Printed in Canada

DEDICATION

I am thankful to Jesus for re-entering my life on January 24, 1984, in a hotel room in Orlando, Florida. For a praying mother, Carol Hamilton, who has never given up on any of her six children to be all God planned for them to be! My husband, Tim, who has given me the freedom to be me. Your love, support, and prophetic insight have brought us to this place for such a time as this, and I am grateful. To all who will read, be encouraged and grow into the person God created you to be. Thank you, for this is the reason I live to see all be motivated by His Love!

Delight yourself also in the Lord, And He shall give you the desires of your heart.

—Psalm 37:4, nkjv

CONTENTS

	Foreword	1
1	Do You Believe?	3
2	Living a Life of Balance	5
3	Me, Not Good? Who Said So?	7
4	No Matter What You Face, Walk in Grace	9
5	The Blessing in Your Offering	11
6	Storms of Life	13
7	In Light of Eternity, Does It Really Matter?	15
8	In the Midst of Your Battle, Remember His Mercy Endures Forever!	17
9	Sheila's ABCs of Who You Are in Christ	19
10	Becoming All You Were Created to Be!	20
11	God's Enduring Love Will Never Fail You When You Place Your Trust in Him!	22
12	Trust God's Seed in Time of Need	24
13	Know One's Heart Before You Judge Their Actions	27
14	Transform Your Life into His Mission	29
15	Live, for This Is a New Day!	31
16	God Has You Covered!	33
17	God Loves You!	35
18	Run the Race, Don't Lose Your Place	37
19	Living the Good Life, in the Here and Now!	39
20	Changing of Times, God Will Keep Your Mind!	41
21	Are You Living in the Now, Trusting God No Matter What?	43
22	Don't Feed It and It Can't Live!	45
23	He Who Began a Good Work Will Not Quit!	47
24	Step Up to the Call to Avoid the Fall	50
25	If You Only Knew Who You Are	52
26	God Will Go Beyond Your Understanding	55
27	Give the Devil Something to Fear!	57
28	Living in the Center of God's Will, Will Produce God Life	59
29	There are No Plaids in God: Detecting the Grey Areas in Your Life	61

30	Are You Running the Race or Is the Race Running You?	64
31	Cast All Your Cares on Him, Who Is the Burden Bearer	66
32	Forgiveness—a Powerful Force!	68
33	You Can Depend on God	72
34	Let God's Love Shine!	74
35	Peace Is Yours Today; Don't Forfeit It!	76
36	What Have You Put on the Shelf?	79
37	Have You Learned to Live in Captivity?	82
38	God Sets Your Worth; You Are the Apple of His Eye	84
39	If Money Can Fix It, You Don't Have a Problem	86
40	Trusting Christ Before the Crisis	88
41	Do I Trust God, No Matter What?	91
42	Turn Your Pain into Ministry—Will You Trust Me?	93
43	How True Are You to Your Relationship to God?	96
44	Put Yourself in Their Shoes	99
45	Don't Fight Like the World; Fight With the Word	101
46	An Empty Heart Is a Good Place to Start!	103
47	Time Always Tells the Truth!	106
48	Trust Is Produced in God's Presence	108
49	Praying for Your Spouse	112
50	God's Extreme Makeover: Allowing God to Transform You	115
51	Where You Compare, You Will Compete!	118
52	The Power of Your Words	120
53	Defeating Fear and Doubt	122
54	A Doubter's Traits	124
55	When Life Deals Us the Unexpected, Follow the Still Voice of God!	127
56	Adversity: God's Tool to Refine Us!	129
57	Hidden Roots Produce Bad Fruit in the Heart!	133
58	Do You Need a Spiritual Tune-Up?	137
59	Praying What's On God's Heart	139
60	Don't Allow Man to Define What God Designed	143
	Notes	145
	About the Author	146
	Contact the Author	148

MOTIVATED BY LOVE MINISTRIES
Vision Statement

Growing people in spirit, soul and body.
Reaching into the Word of God
to bring maturity and encouragement
Edifying God's people to be all
He created them to be.

FOREWORD

Write a book? Me? That is what the prophet would say. I looked behind me to see who she was speaking to, but it was not someone else it was me. Then she proceeded to say not only a book but books that would be published and taken around the world for His glory. Me write a book? You see, I had really never believed I could accomplish anything in my life that would make a difference in others. That night in 1987, God had the prophet talk directly to me and the desire birthed a seed in my heart. Little did I know a few years ago when God had me start what I thought to be an e-devotional that it would take on book form and now be in print! God is an amazing God!

December, 1958: I was born one of six children; my father became an alcoholic due to a terrible work accident that would leave him crippled for the rest of his life. My mother (Mama) is a praying woman and she knew what it meant to tarry before the Lord and see breakthrough before it was popular and was called intercession. It took me many years to realize our family was what society would call "dysfunctional". Funny, we thought it was normal for Daddy to get drunk and for Mama to pray until he got home safe and sound.

Unfortunately, many times alcohol wins, and for Daddy it almost destroyed our family; but God! God can take our mistakes and make miracles of them if we will allow Him to do so. Prayer changed our lives and God eventually gave us our Daddy back and we were able to start a new life in Naples, Florida.

I was eleven years old when we moved to Naples. By this time I had almost died three times, from pneumonia to being in a horsing accident that would leave me with a cracked skull, brain concussion, and unconscious for seven days and eight nights, and in the hospital for more than three weeks. When the doctor said there was no hope, Mama and her prayer group started praying. With a praying Mother, Satan would not win!

I am here today to tell you I am a product of what seems to be dysfunction, but God is a God of function and regeneration when He is the center of your life and love. No matter what you face, no matter what comes your way, allow God to show you through His Word how to overcome. He will carry and see you through. Selah's from God are real-life experiences where God proves Himself over and over to me through showing me His Word working in my life even when it seemed impossible. He was there.

As you read these real-life experiences and see a real God and His Word applied to the situations, I hope you find trust and strength in the love of God. He will never leave you nor forsake you. Jesus desires to take every word and turn them into supernatural revelation so that you will be more than an overcomer through His love, blood, and cross.

"You have a book in you." That is what the prophet said. I pray you will find inside of yourself a greater purpose and plan for your life, and that each seed that has been planted within your spirit will come to harvest with great fruit and seed for the building of God's kingdom and others' benefit. Never doubt God's desire to speak not only to you, but through you for His glory.

Selah from God: what some may call worthless, God calls priceless!

— 1 —

DO YOU BELIEVE?

So a man thinks, so He will be.

In the world today, we are bombarded with information from many different sources: social media, radio, television, school, church, books, and magazines, to name a few.

It has been said and widely accepted that "knowledge is power," but with so many sources of knowledge and information out there, how can we be certain we're choosing our knowledge base wisely?

From what sources do you draw your knowledge? The way you answer that question should provide great insight into what you believe about life, God, and your circumstances.

God gave us the unique ability to reason and choose our thought pattern unlike any of His other creations. Because thoughts and beliefs exist before actions, we know our individual thought life leads the way to our individual behaviors. God gave us the free will to think and believe however we choose.

> So now you can pick out what's true and fair, find all the good trails! Lady Wisdom will be your close friend, and Brother Knowledge your pleasant companion. Good Sense will scout ahead for danger, Insight will keep an eye out for you. They'll keep you from making wrong turns, or following the bad directions of those who are lost themselves and can't tell a trail from tumbleweed.
> —Proverbs 2:9, the message

Webster's defines knowledge as "knowing something with familiarity gained through experience or association." God's desire is that we would be filled with His knowledge, that we would be familiar with Him, experience Him, and associate with Him through His Word, and therefore guard us against knowledge sources that could harm His plan for our lives.

Selahs from God

As Solomon points out in Proverbs, our deepest knowledge will directly shape who we become.

> For as he thinks in his heart, so is he.
> —Proverbs 23:7

1. What do you think about?
2. Do you believe the Word of God?
3. Is the Bible your main source of direction and cause?
4. Do you believe God is in control no matter what is going on around you, good or bad?

When you truly seek the knowledge of God, Jesus, and the power of the cross, you can rest in His Word and promises for your life; He has the power to work in all things according to His Word.

> But seek first the kingdom of God and His righteousness, and all these things shall be added to you.
> —Matthew 6:33

If you believe that knowledge is power, then please choose your knowledge source wisely!

> Jesus said to him, "If you can believe, all things *are* possible to him who believes."
> —Mark 9:23, NKJV

2

LIVING A LIFE OF BALANCE

> When we worship the right way, God doesn't stir us up into confusion; he brings us into harmony. This goes for all the churches—no exceptions.
>
> —1 Corinthians 14:33, The Message

A LIFE OF BALANCE; a life of peace; a life of order; do those phrases stir a longing deep inside you? Have you gotten to the point that your to-do lists have lists? Then, to make matters even more frustrating, you can't find your list. I heard it put this way by one of my favorite pastors: "Do you feel like you are stuck in the cul-de-sac of life? Are you on the wheel of life, going nowhere?"

Yes, I have been there: stuck in the cul-de-sac of life without different results. Doing the same thing day after day but expecting different results has been called insanity! For many years my husband, Tim, and I lived on a cul-de-sac; our children were allowed to play there. They would ride their bikes because there were only three homes on the cul-de-sac. All the neighbors had children, so we all knew they were there and they were safe. We also knew they could go nowhere from there. When they were small, they rode their bikes very happily, until they figured out that they were going nowhere.

Like our children, I too came to a point that I became so tired of going in circles and getting nowhere that I was desperate enough to ask God for help. Today's verse reminds me that disorder or confusion is not of God. Our God is a God of peace and order. Does this mean we never have hard times or bad things go on in our lives? No. It just means in the midst of the storms of life we have God's mind and His peace as a director of balance.

God sent His Son for our lives to have godly order, in spite of chaos. I began to seek God's help in taking a hard right out of the cul-de-sac of nowhere, in order to realize I could enjoy the peace and balance God intends for me by choosing His plans for me over the world's demands on me.

Going nowhere will wear you out and keep you from doing well for Christ. God is calling you to His presence to fill you with His power and give you direction to move out of the cul-de-sac to move from just existing to a life of power, love, and movement. A life of living for His glory. Will you say yes?

How does one say yes? The first step in getting out of the mediocrity cul-de-sac of nowhere is giving up time from sleep to be with the King of Glory. Say yes to a daily prayer time each morning before you meet your family or leave for work.

Pray, communicate with God, and then obey His word and direction for this day. Let yesterday's failures go, and obey today what God has for you to do. Sacrificing sleep was not at all what I wanted to do. It wasn't that I didn't want to meet with the Lord each day; I just really loved to sleep. However, this has been the best thing for me, providing the most effective tool I have in bringing a holy balance to my life.

Meeting with God, having His plan, and obeying it will put your mind at ease. With the sacrifice you are willing to make, God allowed the truth of Psalm 127:26 to settle in your heart: "He gives sleep to those He loves." Let it settle in your heart and life too.

Rest assured, He loves you. Remember He sent His Son to die so you would have eternal life. With that same love, He will bless you with sleep especially when you give it up for Him.

Obedience is the key to having the peace of God. When you have done it His way, at the end of your day, you will lay you head down on your pillow knowing you've honored God. Obedience brings peace of mind and rest you will cherish.

> All who seek the Lord shall find him and shall praise his name. Their hearts shall rejoice with everlasting joy.
> —PSALM 22:26, TLB

~ 3 ~

ME, NOT GOOD? WHO SAID SO?

> Then God saw everything that He had made, and indeed it was very good. So the evening and the morning were the sixth day.
>
> —Genesis 1:31

WE ARE LIVING in a day when many are asking, "What is good?" The Word of God tells me that there is nothing created for mere show. The aim of God in all His modes and works is the highest good to all His creatures. That includes you and me!

Me, not good? Who said so? God made everything, and when He did, He said it was good. Man was one of the things God created, and He proclaimed him good.

> And the Lord God said, "It is not good that man should be alone; I will make him a helper comparable to him."
>
> —Genesis 2:18

God caused man to fall into a deep sleep and He made for him a helpmate that would come from his side to be a companion. Man and woman lived in the Garden of Eden where they were to tend to it, walk, and live with God in the cool of the day. Satan with his evil plan tried to destroy what God created to be good from the very beginning.

If you are born again and have received Christ, you no longer have to live under your parents' DNA but that of God Almighty and His Son Jesus Christ, He who redeemed you from the curse of sin and death. You are a new creation because of the cross at Calvary, redeemed to God's goodness.

When you received Jesus as your Savior, you were redeemed to His image and goodness. You were once a sinner but now you are born again into the family of the only true God. You are His child and He is your Father. You have a new identity in God's Book of

Life. You are reconciled back to the Spirit of God and His original creation of man in the garden where He called him good.

God's Spirit is not just good, but great, gracious, and merciful to all His children. He is a loving Father and He will not fail you, regardless of how good or bad you may be. He loves all of His children the same. He sent His only begotten Son that you may be called a child of God. It is time for the body of Christ to stand their ground and declare, as the apostle Paul did, "My goodness is as filthy rags, but in Christ and Christ alone will I boast." One's goodness is not to be judged by one's actions, but in whom you have believed, Jesus Christ.

Don't allow man or Satan to steal your security in Christ and His goodness. Cast down any thought or imagination that would try to bring your soul (mind, will, and emotions) down to discard what the Spirit desires to do in you. Words that do not edify or encourage you to be more like God and the original image of man in the garden can steal from the power of God in your life. Ask God to show you if there is any place in your heart that needs to be reconciled to Christ. Repent, be restored, and move on.

Praise God for who you are in Him; give Him glory for what He has already done in your life and is yet to do. When you are grateful to God for all the positive and negative things in your life, you defuse Satan and his power in your life. Satan has no truth in him and can only tell you lies, so don't receive anything from him.

No curse of man or Satan can live where you speak God's Word. Give Him praise and allow Him to do only what He can do in you. Let God heal what needs to be healed, fill what needs to be filled, and restore what needs to be restored. Only God's goodness can abide where His love, Word, and will are obeyed.

Remember, you are of God!

> For by Him all things were created that are in heaven and that are on earth, visible and invisible, whether thrones or dominions or principalities or powers. All things were created through Him and for Him.
> —COLOSSIANS 1:16

— 4 —

NO MATTER WHAT YOU FACE, WALK IN GRACE

> But He gives a greater grace. Therefore it says, "God is opposed to the proud, but gives grace to the humble."
>
> —JAMES 4:6, NASU

IN MY LIFE of ministry, I have seen many people (even myself) try to climb the positional "ladder" instead of focusing on a personal relationship with God. It's as though the "good ol' boy mentality" has crept into the church: "If you help promote me to the position I desire, then I will help you get the position you want."

Nowhere in the Bible does God ask this of His servants! In fact, the Bible instructs us to be God pleasers, not pleasers of man. Consider Paul's words:

> Obviously, I'm not trying to win the approval of people, but of God. If pleasing people were my goal, I would not be Christ's servant.
>
> —GALATIANS 1:10, NLT

Grace is given when the people of God accept their life position as He provides it, even if it isn't exactly what they thought they wanted for themselves. They trust God to fulfill His promises as they respond to His calling (not their own!) in humility for His glory.

> So in everything, do to others what you would have them do to you, for this sums up the Law and the Prophets.
>
> —MATTHEW 7:12, NIV

In other words, be kind to others and help them because it's the right thing to do, not because you want something in return. Jesus never promotes the "If you scratch my back, I'll scratch yours" system. Yet by His own example, He does desire to teach us how to put Him in first place.

Jesus said, "Anyone who wants to be first must be the very last, and the servant of all." To anyone who has not received grace, this paradox seems wrong and downright unfair. After all, by the world's standard, if we want to be first, we scratch and claw our way to the top and perform favors to win favors—we don't willingly step into last place!

Especially in ministry, life is not always fair, and we are appointed by God to humble positions in order to grow. To accept a servant position requires tremendous humility, and humility begins and ends with grace. We must trust God in the greatest of times and in the worst. If we choose to walk in grace, we will see His strength made greater each day, no matter what the day brings.

The grace of God gives you the ability to endure the unendurable, love the unlovable, and serve the undeserved. When we allow God to change us from the inside out through humbly serving others, we learn what it means to walk in grace.

Grace is God's gift through the redemption of His Son's anointing, and it is available for His children throughout all eternity.

Simply ask Him for grace and rest assured that no matter what you face, He will give you the ability to walk in grace.

THE BLESSING IN YOUR OFFERING

> Do not be deceived, God is not mocked; for whatever a man sows, that he will also reap.
> —GALATIANS 6:7

THE SEED YOU sow is the seed you grow! Offerings are different from the tithe. God requires the tithe as an act of obedience in the Christian's life. The offering is an act of our free will to deem something valuable enough to give in to it or support with our freewill funds. God gives us the ability to make, acquire, and control money in our lives. When a person tithes, he or she is displaying belief in God's Word and relationship to Him as Father.

The tithe is commanded by God (Leviticus 27:30); the offering is a choice of your will. Man's will can be a strange phenomenon when it comes to letting go of funds not required by God. A person must decide to release or hold on to his or her seed. We can decide to bless or to hold back. The choice is ours.

The will is centered in the soul of man (the mind, will, and emotions). When God asks of His children to give, He will give more back than one could ever imagine. We should never give out of need, but out of our love for God.

Once one can grasp the power behind the blessing in an offering, he or she will search out ministries to bless. Tithes are needed to operate the church, but the offerings fund ministries and benevolence around the world. It is not about a natural return but the supernatural change in lives!

I pray today you will see the blessing of tithing and freewill offerings in your life. You are invited by God to invest into the kingdom of God, to share in spreading the Good News and changing lives around the world.

But seek first the kingdom of God and His righteousness, and all these things shall be added to you.

—MATTHEW 6:33

The benefit in the blessing of the offering:

- It's your choice to exercise your free will to God's will to invest in ministries locally, regionally, and eternally.
- Gives testimony of your faith in God to give you the ability to make, monitor, and distribute funds back to God and charities around the world.
- Displays your confidence in ministries which minister to you and others.
- Makes you a partner with God and others to build the kingdom of God universally.

May the blessing of offering extend far beyond what any one of us could ever imagine or think! As we seek first His kingdom and righteousness, may our storehouse be full to bless, extend the love of Jesus, and bring the light of Christ to a lost and hurting world!

May the blessing of an offering go on forever with eternal seeds until Christ's glorious return!

6

STORMS OF LIFE

> If you will look through the storms of life, you will find the Son of God!
>
> We don't yet see things clearly. We're squinting in a fog, peering through a mist. But it won't be long before the weather clears and the sun shines bright! We'll see it all then, see it all as clearly as God sees us, knowing him directly just as he knows us!
>
> —1 Corinthians 13:12, THE MESSAGE

LIFE DOESN'T ALWAYS give us what we planned. Storms of life don't always come with a warning. When we take what has been given, determined to find God's will in the center of it all, then we will find it. No matter what we are facing, when we determine to find God, then that is exactly who we will find. No matter the storm we are going through, God will never leave nor forsake us. Many times in the middle of the storm we leave Him, and we forsake Him, but God never leaves us. Quite an amazing thing!

No matter what we have done or not done, God still loves us. No matter if we are good or bad, God still loves us. No matter if we measure up to His standards or no standard at all, He still loves us. When we take a step back and look at God, there is no losing with Him. If you are going through a storm at this time in your life, look to God.

Natural storms are made by nature. Spiritual storms can be made from disobedience, tests, or just life itself. Sometimes there are warnings we can heed that a storm is approaching. Other times a storm just comes up due to pressure in the atmosphere—natural or spiritual. The best way to deal with the storms of life is with the Word of God.

If you are going through a storm of life right now and you don't see things clearly, look to God and His Word. If you are in the center of God's will, look to God, for in the quiet times of life you can learn in His peace as much as in the storms.

Life is like a stormy sea. Sometimes you have to get out of the boat and walk on water to get to where you want to go. You may start out feeling fear, but if in truth, you obeyed God's voice, your faith will force out fear. When we obey God and His Word, we will see His life lived through us. Each time you obey Him, you become confident in the God of your faith, His Word, and most of all His ways.

There is not a human being alive who does not have storms of life come their way. Always remember in the midst of life's storms, just like Jesus calmed the storm for His disciples, He will calm the storm for you as you continue to put your trust in Him.

> For they all saw Him and were troubled. But immediately He talked with them and said to them, "Be of good cheer! It is I; do not be afraid."
>
> —MARK 6:50

In your weakest place of faith as you put your trust in God, you are growing in Jesus and His Word each day.

7

IN LIGHT OF ETERNITY, DOES IT REALLY MATTER?

> To everything there is a season, a time for every purpose under heaven.
>
> —ECCLESIASTES 3:1

I CAN REMEMBER BACK when our daughter was around thirteen years old. She did not want to clean her room. I was always cleaning and thought my children should learn the value of having a clean room, in order to set the life desire for a clean and orderly home in the future. I had given her and our son ample time to clean. I went into her room to find she had done nothing. I went into a "holy hissy"! You might not be southern, so let me explain.

What is a "hissy"? It is a fit of rage of screaming and throwing things. Now a "holy hissy" is doing the same as before but all in the name of God! In the midst of my hissy, God spoke to me: "In light of eternity, does it really matter?" In midstream of my flurry of words, I stopped and heard the voice of God so clear. I turned to my daughter and said, "It doesn't matter in light of eternity." She looked as if a ghost had just entered me, and it did, but it was the Holy Ghost. From that day on, I never had to ask her to clean her room. She saw the hand of God move in my heart and it changed hers.

Too many times, we work for temporal things, which will someday fade away and have no eternal reproduction. But when God speaks, He always produces life and change. Is what you are doing today producing the likeness of God? In light of eternity, does it really matter? Temporal things can be used to show God's power if our intentions for them are correct. Even if we are not acting godly, God can use them for His glory if we only listen and obey His voice. In light of eternity does it really matter?

Selahs from God

By the way, a hissy, even a holy hissy, is never the way to get a teenager to do anything, but if you do so, at least you can be thankful God can use the foolish to make a difference in eternity.

We are assured and know that [God being a partner in their labor] all things work together and are [fitting into a plan] for good to and for those who love God and are called according to [His] design and purpose.

—Romans 8:28, AMP

8

IN THE MIDST OF YOUR BATTLE, REMEMBER HIS MERCY ENDURES FOREVER!

> Oh, give thanks to the LORD, for He is good! For His mercy endures forever. Oh, give thanks to the God of gods! For His mercy endures forever. Oh, give thanks to the Lord of lords! For His mercy endures forever: to Him who alone does great wonders, for His mercy endures forever.
> —PSALM 136:1–4

> Be sober, be vigilant; because your adversary the devil walks about like a roaring lion, seeking whom he may devour.
> —1 PETER 5:8

WHEN ONE IS faced with attacks from the devil, it is important to remember God has given us everything we need to overcome Satan, the world, and the temptation of it! Jesus and His Word will be the power and weapon needed to see the victory prevail.

The *TouchPoint Bible* says, "In order to be effective on the battlefield a soldier must be both well trained and properly equipped. The warrior must be alert for surprise attacks; so it is in our spiritual battle with Satan. Determined to destroy our faith by leading us into sin and discouragement, Satan attacks with blatant temptation and deceptive lies. The Bible teaches that the best weapon for this warfare is the Word of God and prayer."[1]

This is important. No matter what happens, God's faithfulness will prevail over evil and strengthen you so that you can endure after such a time as this, His mercy will endure for you.

In the midst of the battle, remember Sheila's Seven Ways to Victory:

Selahs from God

1. I must determine to do all my warfare through Christ and His Word.

2. I must realize it not my job to do God's job; it's my ministry to be a servant of God in spite of the circumstances around me.

3. I must trust the same faith that brought salvation to me, to be the same faith that will bring victory in the middle of life's battles.

4. I must determine to give God the glory no matter what my natural eyes may see or hear.

5. I must keep my eyes on the goal of Jesus, to display faith, hope, and love, for the greatest of these is *love*!

6. I must be confident in Christ that I can do *all* things through Him that gives me strength.

7. I must remember that the joy of the Lord is my strength!

I can do all things through Christ who strengthens me.
—Philippians 4:13

9

SHEILA'S ABCS OF WHO YOU ARE IN CHRIST

Accepted.. Eph. 1:6
Baptized into Christ Jesus ....Rom. 6:3
Children of Promise..Gal. 4:28
Dead to Sin... 1 Pet. 2:24
Empowered by God ....Eph. 3:20
Fishers of Men..Mark 1:17
God's Beloved..Rom. 1:7
Holy.. Heb. 3:1
Intercessor ....Isa. 53:12
Joint Heirs with Christ... Gal. 4:7
Kingdom Citizens...Phil. 3:20
Light of the World ....John 1:4
Ministers of Reconciliation .... 2 Cor. 5:18
New Creatures..2 Cor. 5:17
One with Him ....Gal. 3:28
Partakers of the Divine Nature .... 2 Pet. 1:4
Quickened Spirit... Eph. 2:1,5
Royal Priesthood .... 1 Pet. 2:9
Servants of the Most High God........................... Acts 16:17
Temple of the Holy Spirit..................................... 1 Cor. 6:19
Under the Blood ....Rev. 1:5
Victorious ....1 Cor. 15:57
Walking in the Newness of Life ....Rom. 6:4
Xtra Special to God ....John 3:16,17
You are Saved by Grace Through Faith............... Rom. 5:1,2
Zealous for God...Num. 25:13; Prov. 22:6

Special thank you to my sister in Christ and friend, Catherine Latimer, for co-authoring these "ABC's of Who You Are In Christ" in 1990.

10

BECOMING ALL YOU WERE CREATED TO BE!

Train up a child in the way he should go and when he is old he will not depart from it.

—Proverbs 22:6

When my children were young, they sometimes would struggle with school, relationships, and life in general. As I was in prayer one day, the Lord directed me to write down five questions to ask them as an affirmation to who they were in Him—questions which they could ask themselves during the day, which would remind them they were children of the Most High God because at an early age each one of them had received Jesus in their hearts.

Question one was their name. Why their name? Your name reminds you where you came from, reminds you of your heritage, and gives you a sense of stability. Each day I would ask my children these five questions. Their day was built on the Word of God, who they are in the kingdom of God, and what the rights of a child of the King are. These questions have been used by thousands to become stronger not only as children but as adults to become all God created them to be!

- Question: Who are you?

- Answer: (Name) _____, a King's kid!

- Question: What do you have?

- Answer: The mind of Christ (1 Cor. 2:16)

Becoming All You Were Created to Be!

- Question: What can you do?

- Answer: All things through Christ who gives me strength (Phil. 4:13)

- Question: Who protects you?

- Answer: Jesus and His angels (Ps. 91:11)

- Question: Who is your great teacher?

- Answer: The Holy Spirit (1 Cor. 2:12–13)

Father, in the name of Jesus give angels charge over and keep (Name) _____ this day; put a guard at the gates to protect him/her from this world's evil and a place a guard at the gate of his/her mouth so that he/she will speak only when it is the correct time; bring to his/her remembrance all he/she or she needs to know, that (Name) _____ may be the best student possible, and make him/her a light in the darkness today.

In Jesus' name, Amen.

Psalm 91; Psalm 141:3; John 14:16; Matthew 5:16
Pray over children with any attention deficit problems. God is the restorer of all!

~ 11 ~

GOD'S ENDURING LOVE WILL NEVER FAIL YOU WHEN YOU PLACE YOUR TRUST IN HIM!

> Give thanks to the LORD, for he is good! His faithful love endures forever.
>
> —PSALM 136:1, NLT

LIFE DOES NOT always turn out as one may have planned—but one thing I can assure you, God's love endures. No matter what has happened, is happening, or will happen, the one thing you and I can be promised is that God's love has never changed.

The cost for His love will always be the same: His Son's life. Everything you need is in the work of the cross, His love, and most of all the power of the Holy Spirit. God's love covers a multitude of sins. It casts out all fear. Love is what gave you and me eternal life. There is nothing God's love cannot take care of when we trust Him.

> For I am persuaded that neither death nor life, nor angels nor principalities nor powers, nor things present nor things to come, nor height nor depth, nor any other created thing, shall be able to separate us from the love of God which is in Christ Jesus our Lord.
>
> —ROMANS 8:38–39

Nothing and no one can stop God's love from coming to you. There is not a sin or an action you can do which would stop Him from loving you. Even the worst of sinners God still loves, for while we were all yet sinners He loved us. There is no excuse man can ever use that will give good reason for God not to love him.

Trusting a loving God is one of the surest ways of having true love in your heart, mind, and spirit. God is love; His love takes away all fear; His love is what sent His Son, Jesus Christ, to the cross of Calvary. I encourage you: live to love, love to forgive, and choose never to forget His eternal love is unconditional, and it will endure.

May all you ever do have one motive and one alone: to be motivated by His love! For Jehovah is good; His lovingkindness endureth for ever, and his faithfulness unto all generations.

—Psalm 100:5, asv

12

TRUST GOD'S SEED IN TIME OF NEED

> Now He who supplies seed to the sower and bread for food will supply and multiply your seed for sowing and increase the harvest of your righteousness.
>
> —2 Corinthians 9:10, nasu

Don't allow the cares of this life to steal the strength of your seed which God has implanted within you.

In times of need, trust your seed. God has not changed His mind on why He sent His Son to Calvary; it was for you and me! It was for you and me to live in the abundant life His Son, Jesus Christ, provided upon the cross of Calvary. In your time of need you need to bring to remembrance whose seed lives in your heart as a child of God: His Son's!

Life brings challenges, some of which we expect and others we don't! We all can worship when harvest is happening, especially when you can touch, taste, and see God. On the contrary, what about when you can't hear His voice and it seems the walls are all closing in on you? This is when you must trust God's seed within!

Sadly, in times of need we Christians forget to trust our seed which we have planted in the fertile soil of God's kingdom. Many times believers love what God has provided rather than God Himself! Maturity doesn't come because things are always good. Spiritual maturity comes when one trusts God in the good times or in the tough times. Trust the seed of God in you.

I can recall when my children were teenagers. They were very well behaved children. They really never gave my husband and me any trouble. They have never been on drugs, nor have they ever been arrested. Truly we were and have been blessed by our children. But there was a time my daughter got involved with a young man from school and she thought she was in love. She had to be on the phone with the young man, and we could go nowhere because she had to be home to get his call.

I will never forget. One night she and I got into a terrible fight. She was moving out and going to Mema's house where she could talk to her boyfriend. She was in love and they were going to be married. She was only fifteen years of age, the young man had never been to our home, and she was not allowed to date. But she was in love and she was going to marry him.

My heart was truly broken; I knew my mother would not let her go to her home. I took a walk with my husband, and we talked it over and decided to have the young man over. I was praying the next day and asked God, "What do I do?" I heard in my spirit, "Trust your seed." Trust my seed? What kind of answer is that—*trust your seed*? As I pondered what God had said, He revealed to me I had trained my children up in the way they should go and when they are old, they will not depart.

God instructed me what to do that evening and to do only what He said to do. My husband and I were in agreement to do as the Lord directed. Needless to say, it only took about fifteen minutes for our daughter to realize she was not in love, she did not want to get married, and ask herself, Who is this person sitting at our table? I don't know him at all.

As Christians, we plant seeds of righteousness in our families, our churches, our employment, and our friends, tithes, offerings, and missions. When you are in need, ask God to bring a harvest to the seeds you planted expecting no return. You planted them because you love God, His Son, and being in the family of God. In times of need, whether it is spiritual, personal, or financial, if you have planted into God's kingdom, then He will be faithful to see you through your times of need too!

In times of triumph, it is easy to trust God. What about times of tragedy; do you trust God then? Do you believe in the seed He has planted? Call your seed to harvest that God may get all the glory. And you too, like Paul, may say in time of need or plenty, "I will trust You, Lord."

Selahs from God

> Sow with a view to righteousness, Reap in accordance with kindness; break up your fallow ground, for it is time to seek the Lord until He comes to rain righteousness on you.
> —Hosea 10:12, NASU

~ 13 ~

KNOW ONE'S HEART BEFORE YOU JUDGE THEIR ACTIONS

> Let my heart be blameless regarding Your statutes, that I may not be ashamed.
> —Psalm 119:80, NKJV

BE KINDER THAN necessary to all you meet. You don't know the battle they are in. You may have the answer to their prayers within.

> Stop judging others, and you will not be judged.
> —Matthew 7:1, NLT

Others will treat you as you treat them. Whatever measure you use in judging others, it will be used to measure how you are judged. Not one person alive today can say he or she is worthy of judging another's sin or actions here on this earth.

> For all have sinned and fallen short of the glory of God.
> —Romans 3:23

Christian or non-Christian! As Christians, we are not called to point out each other's faults, but to edify, build up and encourage.

May the body of Christ become restorers of broken bridges, menders of broken lives, and guides for those who need to find their way to Christ! Days before my daddy passed away (December 25, 1997), he said something I have never forgotten. He and I were talking about all he had accomplished; then he said something really sad to me. He said, "It is a real shame my six children never got to know me as a person." Many times we only know others by what they do or by their titles. But do we really know them?

The cancer had by this time taken its toll on his body. At

sixty-seven years old, he would die. Unfortunately, I never really got to know my daddy as a person, the person he so longed for his children to know.

My daddy's statement made a lasting impact on me! He longed for someone to know him, not what he had accomplished. In Philippians 3, Paul longed to know Christ—not just the work of the cross, but to know Him! Know people by their hearts, not their actions.

> [For my determined purpose is] that I may know Him [that I may progressively become more deeply and intimately acquainted with Him, perceiving and recognizing and understanding the wonders of His Person more strongly and more clearly], and that I may in that same way come to know the power outflowing from His resurrection [which it exerts over believers], and that I may so share His sufferings as to be continually transformed [in spirit into His likeness even] to His death, [in the hope]
> —PHILIPPIANS 3:10, AMP

The two men on the crosses at Calvary (Luke 23:39–43) with Jesus were criminals, yet Jesus did not speak to them as criminals. He spoke to them as men in the same plight that He was in, with mercy.

One rejected Jesus. The other recognized Jesus as the true Messiah. Jesus was accused of wrongful deeds, yet He did not return evil for evil. Jesus spoke to the second criminal with compassion, love, and hope. Jesus assured him he would be with Him in spite of his crimes. Why? Jesus knew him by his heart, not his actions.

> For the word of God is living and powerful, and sharper than any two-edged sword, piercing even to the division of soul and spirit, and of joints and marrow, and is a discerner of the thoughts and intents of the heart.
> —HEBREWS 4:12

— 14 —

TRANSFORM YOUR LIFE INTO HIS MISSION

> I thank my God upon every remembrance of you, always in every prayer of mine making request for you all with joy, for your fellowship in the gospel from the first day until now, being confident of this very thing, that He who has begun a good work in you will complete it until the day of Jesus Christ.
> —PHILIPPIANS 1:3–6

THE APOSTLE PAUL was writing to those he loved from a prison of uncertainty, yet he did not let his surroundings change his mind about his God. Prison became a place of ministry; chains became a place of evangelism, where prisoners were transformed and jailers converted.

Why? Paul did not let the bad things of life spoil the mission of Christ he had been called to. In truth, it was a place where he would see the benefit of the bad for the furtherance of the gospel of the Lord Jesus Christ. Paul was not about his ministry, but the mission of Christ, which he had been called to fulfill. Ministry or mission, the Great Commission is to seek those who are lost, to introduce them to a real and living Jesus. Paul did not live in regret or rejection even while in prison or even facing death. Either he was crazy or he really did believe no matter what he faced that Jesus and the Holy Spirit were going to see him through. Paul was confident of his God! In fact, he said, "I am confident in this one thing, He who has began a good work will be faithful to complete it, even unto death." (See Philippians 1:6.) The apostle Paul trusted his God, not his surroundings.

We should desire this kind of faith. No matter the circumstance, the rejection, or the persecution, we will not let go of God and His promises to us. For this one thing we truly can be confident in: He is faithful!

I thank God for each of you. I pray you will be called to something bigger than a ministry, for ministries come and go, but the Great Commission in Christ Jesus will live on until the day of Christ's return. As your life is transformed into His mission for His glory and love to expand the kingdom of God, does what you're doing for Christ today have eternal value?

> "For I know the plans I have for you," says the Lord. "They are plans for good and not for disaster, to give you a future and a hope. In those days when you pray, I will listen."
> —Jeremiah 29:11–12, NLT

─ 15 ─

LIVE, FOR THIS IS A NEW DAY!

> Who redeems your life from destruction, who crowns you with lovingkindness and tender mercies, who satisfies your mouth with good things, so that your youth is renewed like the eagle's.
>
> —PSALM 103:4–5

EACH DAY HUMANS are given a new day, a new dawn, to start fresh in their lives. The world does not have this hope as Christians do. Yet many times, if you look at people, you cannot distinguish between saved or unsaved. They both respond and act the same way in the same circumstances. Why don't Christians act any different? Because we as Christians have not learned to live through faith out of our spirit man, rather than our soul realm (mind, will, and emotions).

> Don't copy the behavior and customs of this world, but let God transform you into a new person by changing the way you think. Then you will know what God wants you to do, and you will know how good and pleasing and perfect his will really is.
>
> —ROMANS 12:2, NLT

> Don't become so well-adjusted to your culture that you fit into it without even thinking. Instead, fix your attention on God. You'll be changed from the inside out. Readily recognize what he wants from you, and quickly respond to it. Unlike the culture around you, always dragging you down to its level of immaturity, God brings the best out of you, develops well-formed maturity in you.
>
> —ROMANS 12:2, THE MESSAGE

Selahs from God

As Christians, we have a new opportunity each day to live not as the world would live in fear, doubt, and unbelief, but in love, faith, hope, and complete confidence God will not fail us. What worldly customs are you conforming to? Or are you transforming daily by the love, Word, and hope which are in Christ Jesus? It's a new day; start fresh. Do not allow yesterday's pain to steal your joy of living today. Allow God to transform you now in the here and now! Allow His love to flow where you hurt, and His hope to grow where you fear. Choose this day what you will serve!

- Make the choice to live today in the day the Lord has made.
- Choose to rejoice in it! No matter what you're facing, rejoice.
- In every circumstance, renew your mind to the things of God.
- Survey everything you do through the goodness of God, not man.
- Become a life giver! Each day is a gift, and serving is a choice.

The power of the life-giving Spirit has freed you from the power of sin that leads to death.
—Romans 8:2, NLT

And if it seems evil to you to serve the Lord, choose for yourselves this day whom you will serve, whether the gods which your fathers served that *were* on the other side of the River, or the gods of the Amorites, in whose land you dwell. But as for me and my house, we will serve the Lord.
—Joshua 24:15

16

GOD HAS YOU COVERED!

> Blessed is he whose transgression is forgiven, whose sin is covered.
> —Psalm 32:1

I have a great need for Christ; I have a great Christ for my need.
—Charles Haddon Spurgeon (1834–1892)

There is nothing that God has left uncovered! Everything in the life of a Christian is covered through the shed blood of Jesus Christ and His cross. Never feel you're alone, and never believe you have been too bad for God to cover you.

> For nothing is secret that will not be revealed, nor *anything* hidden that will not be known and come to light.
> —Luke 8:17

Whatever you're facing today was covered through the work of the cross of Calvary. All you desire for His glory will and has been paid for in the work of salvation. You do not have to work for it; just trust God, obey His Word, and you will see His glory in your life today.

> You have forgiven the iniquity of Your people; You have covered all their sin.
> —Psalm 85:2

God has you covered; every sin, past, present, and future, every triumph, every victory. In your goodness or your weakness, all you need is in the life of Christ. Trust God; He has you and your life covered.

God covered Adam in the garden when he sinned; He covered

Noah when he was drunk and uncovered. There is nothing in our lives that God will not cover when we call upon His name. Allow the Holy Spirit to heal you where you are in pain. I assure you today, God has you covered!

Do not allow self, Satan, or the systems of this world to remove your covering in Jesus! Love covers a multitude of sins, and God's love casts out all fear. He's got you covered through His Son's love, blood, and cross. You are pure, and you are His!

> There is no fear in love; but perfect love casts out fear, because fear involves torment. But he who fears has not been made perfect in love.
> —1 John 4:18

17

GOD LOVES YOU!

> I love those who love me, and those who seek me early and diligently shall find me.
>
> —PROVERBS 8:17, AMP

I WAS LOOKING FOR something profound to share one day, but nothing came. I asked the Holy Spirit for a direct word, yet nothing came. That morning I went to prayer only to hear, "I love you; I love my people."

I was looking for the profound and found the love of God. Wow, the love of God! God sent His only begotten Son to earth to live, to die, resurrect, and send the Comforter, the Holy Spirit, all because of this love! Love for you and me! A love through Christ Jesus, which nothing can ever separate us from! The love of God that has covered all sin, past, present, and future.

> Do you think anyone is going to be able to drive a wedge between us and Christ's love for us? There is no way! Not trouble, not hard times, not hatred, not hunger, not homelessness, not bullying threats, not backstabbing, not even the worst sins listed in Scripture.
>
> —ROMANS 8:35, THE MESSAGE

His love allowed you and me to come into the family of God, free from all debt, guilt, and shame. Oh, and I was looking for something profound! I believe not only did I find it, but I need His love more today than ever before. Take your time and read this text like you are reading it for the first time. Do not apply it to another, but to you only!

> If I speak in the tongues of men and of angels, but have not love, I am only a resounding gong or a clanging cymbal. If

I have the gift of prophecy and can fathom all mysteries and all knowledge, and if I have a faith that can move mountains, but have not love, I am nothing. If I give all I possess to the poor and surrender my body to the flames, but have not love, I gain nothing. Love is patient, love is kind. It does not envy, it does not boast, it is not proud. It is not rude, it is not self-seeking, it is not easily angered, it keeps no record of wrongs. Love does not delight in evil but rejoices with the truth. It always protects, always trusts, always hopes, always perseveres. Love never fails. But where there are prophecies, they will cease; where there are tongues, they will be stilled; where there is knowledge, it will pass away. For we know in part and we prophesy in part, but when perfection comes, the imperfect disappears. When I was a child, I talked like a child, I thought like a child, I reasoned like a child. When I became a man, I put childish ways behind me. Now we see but a poor reflection as in a mirror; then we shall see face to face. Now I know in part; then I shall know fully, even as I am fully known. And now these three remain: faith, hope and love. But the greatest of these is love.

—1 Corinthians 13:1–13, NIV

Why wait for disappointments to try God? Live in His love, operate in His power, and dwell in the secret place to be loved, sure, and confident. No matter what, you are loved!

18

RUN THE RACE, DON'T LOSE YOUR PLACE

> Therefore, as the elect of God, holy and beloved, put on tender mercies, kindness, humility, meekness, longsuffering; bearing with one another, and forgiving one another, if anyone has a complaint against another; even as Christ forgave you, so you also must do. But above all these things put on love, which is the bond of perfection.
> —COLOSSIANS 3:12–14

WHERE IS YOUR heart today? Where is your mind set? There is so much going on in the world today, it is easy to lose your focus and determination for the things of God. Have you lost your place in the rat race of life? Many have gotten on the wheel of life, just making it through life and to church, which has become mere entertainment rather than a place of true worship. True worship will transform you into God's likeness.

Each day we are given a new chance to start afresh in the things of God. It is time to let the past go and embark on a new journey in the things of God. He never changes. He is always the same. Yet He ever desires us to be more like Him and His character. Is your mind set on the things of God or on the world and its trappings? Even good things can become a trap if our treasures are not stored up in heaven. We need to put on tender mercies every day, and then the world will see the love of God as we go along our paths of life.

God does not look at race, economical status, or DNA, but He looks to see if His Son is in our hearts. The author of Colossians wrote to "put it on," which shows it is a choice—tender mercies, love, kindness, forgiveness. Each morning we get up and we put clothes on; it's a choice what to wear today. If you didn't put clothes on and left home, you would suffer the consequences of not dressing.

It's the same with God. How much of Him are you going to put on today? Each Christian has a free will, and you can choose as much or as little of God as you desire. Your life will be full or it will be empty of God. When you go along in life and lose your place, it may be because you did not fill your mind, will, and emotions with the Word of God and His fruit.

Many start out the race with great intentions. I love Nascar. I never hear the drivers at the beginning of a race say, "We are out here to lose." No, they are all optimistic about winning. Maybe you started out well but now seem hindered from running the race with God as your partner. Who stopped you from getting to the finish line?

You ran well. Who hindered you from obeying the truth?
—GALATIANS 5:7

We do not love, show tender mercies, and forgive by feelings; we do it by faith! Make a choice today to live as if it were your last, and you will see love grow in ways you never thought possible.

Set your mind on things above, not on things on the earth.
—COLOSSIANS 3:2

When we set our minds on things above, we make a difference for His glory and build His kingdom. The world and those around you will know you love them more by your actions than your words! In life's race don't lose your place in God, His love, and most of all His family!

~ 19 ~

LIVING THE GOOD LIFE, IN THE HERE AND NOW!

Not that I speak in regard to need, for I have learned in whatever state I am, to be content.

—PHILIPPIANS 4:11

EARLY IN 2010, Tim and I took some time for rest and relaxation in the Florida Keys. These past few months things in our lives have been more intense than ever before; it seems time together is the first thing we sacrifice in our marriage. Tim loves to fish; if you ask him why he works, he will tell you to take care of his family and be able to go fishing. Tim is a very giving person and loves to do what he does for others out of the sight of man.

I have learned much from my husband and honor him. If you ask him why he does what he does, from donations of time, money, or efforts, he will tell you, "So I can fish with a clear mind and no weights on my life." Tim loves the Lord, his family, and his fishing! If you ask him where he loves to be for vacation or a weekend away, it is always the same answer, "The Florida Keys!"

When down in the Keys there are a few places we like to go out to eat. Lazy Days, where you can take your catch and they will make it to order. Yummy! For breakfast, we go to Mangrove Mike's. When you enter, Mike greets all with, "Good morning, living the good life in the Florida Keys."

The last four years we have become accustomed to Mike greeting his customers with a weird wig or hat with his great saying, "Living the good life in the Florida Keys." The Holy Spirit impressed on my heart this is how more of His children need to be: living the "Good Life" no matter what they are facing!

As Tim and I watched Mangrove Mike, Tim said, "It's amazing

he has opened three new businesses that last year." One of the three has already failed, yet when asked, he still responds, "Living the good life in the Florida Keys."

Did I happen to mention the business that failed was a second restaurant? You would think that if he has one of the most successful restaurants in the Florida Keys, he would succeed in another! Yet Mike has not allowed the economy or his failure to stop his resolve.

Maybe you today have had things that would try to make you feel you are not living the Good Life. The "Good Life" is not money, location, or material things! Jesus came to give life and give it more abundantly. Abundance is not about things but a relationship with Christ.

Living the Good Life does not mean that everything is perfect; living the Good Life should be centered on Christ and His love, and what He did for you on the cross of Calvary, trusting Him to carry you when you can't carry yourself.

Failure should never be the believer's finish line, but the starting place. The Word of God says Jesus learned from the things He suffered. Failure can be a pause in life to consider what has happened, learn from it, repent, and then allow the Holy Spirit to do what only He can do: heal you. Have faith in God's Word. It will not return void to those who put their hope in Him!

It is time to start living the Good Life! Don't wait for it to come to you; create it where you are right now! Enjoy the journey! Join God in what He is doing, and you will see Him in all you do. He loves you. Are you living the God Life to produce the Good Life in Christ?

~ 20 ~

CHANGING OF TIMES, GOD WILL KEEP YOUR MIND!

> You will keep him in perfect peace, whose mind is stayed on You, because he trusts in You.
>
> —Isaiah 26:3

In the days and times in which we live, we must keep our minds fixed on Jesus and His Word. Many times, I hear seasoned believers say they have changed their thoughts on what the Word of God says concerning their lives. If the Word of God convicted you two or twenty years ago, then the Word did not change, your mind did.

God's Word is the same yesterday, today, and forever! We as Christians should not change God's Word to fit into our lifestyles. Jesus Christ gave His life for believers to be conformed into His image, not to fit a lifestyle. In changing times, it is easy to give in under pressure. If you will continue in the Word of God, you will see you serve a faithful God!

Jesus Christ has promised to go with you all the way. No matter what you are facing or going through, He will never forsake or leave you! He promised He would keep you in perfect peace when you keep your mind stayed on Him!

> You will keep him in perfect peace, whose mind is stayed on You, because he trusts in You.
>
> —Isaiah 26:3

Changing of times means you don't change your mind in the middle of conflict. Continue trusting God Almighty. The Word of God says it rains on the just and the unjust. God has never seen the righteous forsaken or His seed out begging for bread. Keep your

Selahs from God

mind stayed on Him! God has not changed; He is faithful! Jesus loves you. Trust Him, and He will support and carry you through!

I have been young, and *now* am old; yet I have not seen the righteous forsaken, nor his descendants begging bread.

—Psalm 37:25

21

ARE YOU LIVING IN THE NOW, TRUSTING GOD NO MATTER WHAT?

> Therefore do not worry about tomorrow, for tomorrow will worry about itself. Each day has enough trouble of its own.
> —Matthew 6:34, niv

MANY TIMES AS Christians, we live in the future instead of the now. When you gave your life to Christ, you received Him as your Lord and Savior. You invited Him to be Lord of your life. He invited you to live your life according to His Word, will, and way. He invited you on a journey with Him to live like He lives, to love like He loves, to be as He is, spirit, soul, and body.

Your journey is not the destination but the path you take along the way to get there. Are you enjoying your journey today? Are you enjoying your life in Christ each step of the way? Your destiny is heaven; your purpose will be fulfilled here on this earth to produce the life in Christ not only in and of yourself, but those that you meet. The question is, are you enjoying your journey in Christ?

A person who is enjoying their journey in Christ is full of love, faith, and fullness of grace for all they meet. They are not worried about climbing the spiritual ladder of acceptance, but are happy just to know God loves them. Out of one's love for God, they obey the Word of God, for in the Word there is life, light, and love in Christ Jesus. Are you living in the now? Are you enjoying your life? Is there something holding you back from stepping into the now of God?

God's desire is for you to share His love and mercy in every area of your life, whatever you may encounter. Living in the past will steal your now! Are you really forgiven? Are you operating in His forgiveness? Forgiveness is a two-way street; with the same measure as you want to be forgiven, so you are to freely give forgiveness to all. Living in the now says, I have released the past to operate in the now for God's glory. He will take care of all that concerns you!

> We are assured and know that [God being a partner in their labor] all things work together and are [fitting into a plan] for good to and for those who love God and are called according to [His] design and purpose. For those whom He foreknew [of whom He was aware of and loved beforehand], He also destined from the beginning [foreordaining them] to be molded into the image of His Son [and share inwardly His likeness], that He might become the firstborn among many brethren.
> —ROMANS 8:28–29, AMP

Survey your life and ask yourself these simple questions:

- Am I enjoying the journey of my life?
- What in my life is causing me pain?
- What has God called me to do for His glory?
- Are temporal things holding me back from the will of God?
- I am really trusting God in the areas that are impossible with man but possible with God?

> Trust (lean on, rely on, and be confident) in the Lord and do good; so shall you dwell in the land and feed surely on His faithfulness, and truly you shall be fed.
> —PSALM 37:3, AMP

Living in the now says, "I trust God! I am going to enjoy the life I have. I will continue in the things of God and continue to see His glory displayed through my life. For all life comes from God. No matter what happens today, everything has to go through God's hands! Because I am a child of the King, I can be assured that all things work together for His glory and my good. In Jesus' name."

~ 22 ~

DON'T FEED IT AND IT CAN'T LIVE!

What you value, you will nurture!

In the day and time in which we live, there is much in the media and advertising about losing weight. The weight-loss business is a booming industry. It's reported by the FDA that Americans spend an estimated $40 billion a year on all types of diet programs and products, including diet foods, diet drinks, and more. An estimated 50 million Americans will go on diets each year.

> May God himself, the God who makes everything holy and whole, make you holy and whole, put you together—spirit, soul, and body—and keep you fit for the coming of our Master, Jesus Christ.
> —1 Thessalonians 5:23, The Message

Yet we cannot neglect the temple of God while setting our minds on the things above. We are to be good stewards of our time, efforts, and resources. If we allow any part of our spirit, soul, or body to be unfit, then we are neglecting some part of what God has asked of us. We are to feed our spirit spiritual food; we are to set our minds on things that are of God; and we are to feed our bodies things that are wholesome and healthy.

> God hasn't invited us into a disorderly, unkempt life but into something holy and beautiful—as beautiful on the inside as the outside.
> —1 Thessalonians 4:7, The Message

Don't feed it, and it won't live; what you want to live, you feed. If there is something in your life today you want to change, then you can do this by not feeding it or changing what you are feeding it to see a different result. This can be done spirit, soul, and body. If you want to change your spiritual attitude, then feed on the Word. If you want to change your mind-set, then activate the presence of God and ask Him, "What do you want from me? I will follow your way." If your temple (human body) needs to come under subjection to the Spirit, then you too can ask God to give you a desire to change habits, and the desire to break that which has taken years to acquire. The amazing thing about God and your body is that it's never too late to start over again. God is so full of grace. He desires us to change, to be more like Him each morning where His mercies are new every day.

Our bodies have memory. If you exercised in the past, when you start again, your body will catch up quickly as you discipline yourself. As you submit to a routine, it will work if you continue steadfast in it. If the temple has not been a priority, then start somewhere! Take a walk up the beach, up your street, or around the mall. Exercise is as much about the mind as it is the body. Whatever you want to live, feed. Make a list of things in your life you desire to see live, grow, and reproduce. Then make a list of things that need to die. What kind of fruit is being produced in your life? Don't feed it, and it will not be able to live. Good or bad, what do you want to live in your life today?

~ 23 ~

HE WHO BEGAN A GOOD WORK WILL NOT QUIT!

Being confident of this, that he who began a good work in you will carry it on to completion until the day of Christ Jesus.

—PHILIPPIANS 1:6, NIV

*S*TAY THE COURSE, *focused on Jesus, and most of all stay in God's Word*!

And I am sure that God, who began a good work within you, will continue his work until it is finally finished on that day when Christ Jesus comes back again.

—PHILIPPIANS 1:6, NLT

"God's promise to continue working in our lives requires perseverance on our part." Perseverance (longsuffering) is a fruit of the Spirit; if you are lacking it, ask God and He will give freely according to the Word of God.

If you don't know what you're doing, pray to the Father. He loves to help. You'll get his help, and won't be condescended to when you ask for it. Ask boldly, believingly, without a second thought. People who "worry their prayers" are like wind-whipped waves. Don't think you're going to get anything from the Master that way, adrift at sea, keeping all your options open. When down-and-outers get a break, cheer!

—JAMES 1:5–10, THE MESSAGE

When waiting on God to move we must remember He knows what we're going through. He sees what is happening, and He can be everywhere at once. He has not forgotten you, He has not forsaken you, He is right here with you! Remember, waiting is a place where you can learn more about God and your relationship with Him than in any other place.

Here are some questions you may want to ask yourself as you are waiting on God:

1. Am I impatient with waiting on God?
2. Do I trust Him to complete what He has promised me?
3. How is that for which you are hoping going to change your life for God and His purpose?
4. In light of eternity, how will this affect not only me but all I will meet for God's glory?
5. Is what I am waiting on temporal or eternal? "Set your mind on things above, not on things on the earth" (Col. 3:2).
6. If what I desire never comes, will I still love Jesus until the end?

When your want overrides your desire for Jesus, self and Satan will always win. The writer of Revelation encourages Christians to keep their eyes on Jesus, *who will reward the faithful, and to obey His Word to the end.* Has what you've been waiting on become an idol in your heart? In the middle of the waiting have you allowed yourself to lose the joy of your salvation?

I am reminded of the apostle Paul, who prayed three times for the thorn in his side to be removed. It never was, but instead of becoming bitter, he wrote thirteen books of the New Testament. *He who began a good work is faithful to finish it!* (Phil. 1:16).When you feel like giving up, remember the glory that awaits you as a child of God.

> Let this encourage you as God's holy people to endure patiently and remain firm to the end, obeying his commands and trusting in Jesus.
> —Revelation 14:12, NLT

Let this encourage you as a godly person to endure persecution patiently and remain firm to the end, obeying His commands and trusting in Jesus.

24

STEP UP TO THE CALL TO AVOID THE FALL

God told Cain, "Satan is waiting right outside the door for you to fall."

> If thou doest well, shalt thou not be accepted? And if thou doest not well, sin lieth at the door. And unto thee shall be his desire, and thou shalt rule over him.
> —Genesis 4:7, kjv

> If you do well, won't you be accepted? And if you don't do well, sin is lying in wait for you, ready to pounce; it's out to get you, you've got to master it.
> —Genesis 4:7, msg

If Satan is watching for you to fall, then God has to be watching for you to step up to the call of the next level of obedience. He is asking you to step up to the call to avoid the fall. Obedience to God will bring Him glory, expand His kingdom, and bless you in the process.

Have you learned to live in captivity, calling it freedom? Pride will keep us in captivity. It will also steal our destiny in God and His purpose for our lives. God's purpose is not about ministry; it is about knowing Him, His Word, and His Holy Spirit. Obedience and prayer will lead us out of bondage into our true promised land.

It is time to examine our hearts to see what is of God or man. Will you take authority over the things that have kept your spirit, soul, and body in captivity? Step up to the call of God and you will see He will make a way where there seems to be no way. He will open doors no man can shut. I heard a pastor years ago say there are usually two lines in a church or ministry service: the prayer line or the pride line.

> Pride goes before destruction, a haughty spirit before a fall.
> —Proverbs 16:18, niv

Step Up to the Call to Avoid the Fall

God is asking you to be honest with yourself, and I promise it is OK to be honest with God. God can handle your sin, your failures, and your secrets, whether it is a fear or a sin; God can handle it! God loves it when you allow Him to restore you in private that He may exalt His divine work in public. He is asking you to spend time with Him in prayer, to talk with Him, to listen and then obey what He desires for you and your life.

You and I do not serve a God of embarrassment; His love is as that of a pure Father; He is full of grace and mercy. He is asking you and me to step up to the call to avoid the fall, but if you fail God, He promises He will pick up the righteous man seven times in one day! He will never let you go, and He does not want to see you fall! He is calling us higher in spirit, soul, and body! Satan may have set you up for the fall, but God set you up for the call.

> Being confident of this very thing, that He who has begun a good work in you will complete it until the day of Jesus Christ.
>
> —PHILIPPIANS 1:6

— 25 —

IF YOU ONLY KNEW WHO YOU ARE

> And Saul said to David, "You are not able to go against this Philistine to fight with him; for you are a youth, and he a man of war from his youth."
>
> —1 SAMUEL 17:33

> David said, "The LORD, who delivered me from the paw of the lion and from the paw of the bear, He will deliver me from the hand of this Philistine." And Saul said to David, "Go, and the LORD be with you!"
>
> —1 SAMUEL 17:37

THE DEVIL WISHES to steal your destiny! David did not look like a Jew, nor did he look like Saul. He was short and small in size; he was not the people's choice. When the prophet Samuel came to Jesse's house looking for the next king, he did not find him. For God had sent Samuel to anoint him. After looking over all of Jesse's sons, Samuel asked, "Do you have any more sons?" Jesse, David's father, replied, "I have a strapping one." Samuel said to go get him. Jesse did not think David was to be king. Even if your father has never approved you or nurtured you, you have a heavenly Father who approves you with all your faults and successes!

You can live in the valley of praise and not have the victory or peace of Jesus. Jesse sends David to feed his brothers and he finds them in a quandary. The brothers had seen Goliath's stature and they were defeated before they went to battle. Goliath had showed them his armor and they compared his size, his weapons, and his skill and decided in their minds the giant had already won.

In his brothers' minds, Goliath had intimidated them into thinking they had already lost. Satan will try to make you think he is bigger than he really is. Most people decide their outcome of the battle before they ever start to fight. Do not lose the battle in your mind before you have ever fought in the natural by the supernatural power of God.

When David came upon his brothers, he did not ask them how big the enemy was; he asked, What do you get if you kill the giant? He was looking toward the prize at the end. No matter how big your own enemy looks, you have to come face to face with it! Throughout time, men have blamed their circumstances on someone else. First, we need to look at our own lives to see if this battle was chosen by God or if it was brought on by sin in our lives. If you are clear on its origin, you can face it through God's forgiveness and grace, and you can win.

God is placing us in positions to say to the devil and his imps (fallen angels) that they have no power and most of all no authority over a child of God! What attitude do you have in the heat of the battle? Do you see victory before you go to war; have you counted the cost and realized all you have to do to win the battle is not give up? Satan has no power when your faith is established in God's Word and blood.

Second Corinthians 10:3–5 (NKJV) says, "For though we walk in the flesh, we do not war according to the flesh. For the weapons of our warfare are not carnal but mighty in God for pulling down strongholds." In the heat of the battle, you can be a wimp or a warrior, a defeatist or a conqueror, a victim or a victor; it's your choice. The devil cannot do anything to you when you have Jesus within you, for God will give you ability to overcome, as His Word says that "greater is He that is in you, than he that is in the world" (1 John 4:4, KJV).

When you know who you are in Jesus, you will not be afraid to tell the devil who he is and where he is going back to! Do not just knock your enemy down, but also make sure he is defeated, dead, and destroyed. Don't allow Satan back into your life. As you trust God and His Word, you will be strengthened to overcome the attacks of the enemy from every side.

You don't have to fight many demons, just the one that has been trying to keep you down. Jesus paid the price on the cross for you and me to win. We only have to believe, receive, put God in His proper place in our hearts, and then tell Satan he has to move out because there is not enough room for Jesus, Satan, and us! God does not cohabitate with Satan and neither should a child of God! You are more than a conqueror. Don't go back to where you have already been healed. Know who you are in Christ; healed, whole, and redeemed!

26

GOD WILL GO BEYOND YOUR UNDERSTANDING

"For My thoughts are not your thoughts, nor are your ways My ways," says the Lord. "For as the heavens are higher than the earth, so are My ways higher than your ways, and My thoughts than your thoughts."

—Isaiah 55:8–9

The Word of God should determine our perspective of life. How can we make sure our perspective is correct? Communication with God by the prayer of faith and according to what the Holy scriptures have told us. We can only get a true perspective through God's Holy Bible. We will get His perspective by spending time not only in His Word but also in His presence!

No matter how long you have been saved, you will never understand God and all His ways! For His ways are higher than ours! Faith is always going to be required, no matter how mature you are in God's kingdom, Word, or will. God's Word goes beyond your understanding in order that He can do His will in your life.

This is why faith is called faith; you can't explain it. As you trust Jesus and the work of the cross, you will see His life manifest and matured through you! Never stop trying to understand His Word and His ways for His glory! God will not keep His will from you, He will give you peace in the middle of gaining understanding.

> Happy is the man who finds wisdom, and the man who gains understanding; for her proceeds are better than the profits of silver, and her gain than fine gold.
>
> —Proverbs 3:13–14

> Let not mercy and truth forsake you; bind them around your neck, write them on the tablet of your heart, and so

find favor and high esteem in the sight of God and man. Trust in the Lord with all your heart, and lean not on your own understanding.

—PROVERBS 3:3–5

We are told not to lean upon our own understanding, but in all ways acknowledge God. Trying to understand God's Word shows your desire to know Him and His ways. Remember, His ways are higher, but this does not mean you do not try to understand them. Maturity is a process by which you will gain access to His power and love; which reveals His character and will.

God's perspective is His Word! God's perspective is to gain wisdom, not to reveal the future, but to reveal the heart of God. For His image to be formed in us, then through us, for His glory! God will hold nothing back from you when you have His perspective and Word living through you. His anointing desires to direct each step you take.

As you step out in faith, it shows you have trusted His Spirit and Word to complete in you what He has called you to for His glory. Faith shows your trust not only in God, but also in His Word. Allow God's perspective to become your reality, and then you will go higher in Him and His Spirit.

~ 27 ~

GIVE THE DEVIL SOMETHING TO FEAR!

> For God hath not given us the spirit of fear; but of power, and of love, and of a sound mind.
> —2 Timothy 1:7, kjv

Speak God's Word; the seed you sow will be the seed you grow!

God is all powerful, and Satan has been defeated. Never forget in whom you trust; when God has control, your life is in God's hands.

> They will see the glory of the Lord, the majesty of our God. Encourage the exhausted, and strengthen the feeble. Say to those with anxious heart, "Take courage, fear not. Behold, your God will come with vengeance; the recompense of God will come, but He will save you."
> —Isaiah 35:2–4, nasu

Christians today are assailed from every side with negative news, thoughts, and happenings. Satan wants our minds assaulted with these, for this is when he can do his best work. As Christians, we are not called to be negative. We are to be life givers with hope and a future in the words we speak.

> As it is written: "I have made you a father of many nations." He is our father in the sight of God, in whom he believed—the God who gives life to the dead and calls into being things that were not.
> —Romans 4:17, niv

God's words created all we see, feel, and enjoy today. Our words have power to create life, light, and love. Our words display what is in our hearts. When pressure is applied, what comes out of our mouths? God, through His Son Jesus, came to give life. We are to be examples of God's love, and as His children should bring forth the love of Jesus in every area of our lives.

What do your words say about your life? What are you doing with the time you have to encourage those around you? If every jot and tittle of your day is kept in God's Book of Life; are you satisfied with what you would read at the end of this day? We are to be givers of life, Christ's life! Are your words life giving; are they edifying to all you meet?

The seed you sow will be the seed you grow.

> For he that soweth unto his own flesh shall of the flesh reap corruption; but he that soweth unto the Spirit shall of the Spirit reap eternal life. And let us not be weary in well-doing: for in due season we shall reap, if we faint not. So then, as we have opportunity, let us work that which is good toward all men, and especially toward them that are of the household of the faith.
> —GALATIANS 6:8–10, ASV

What you plant today may be the harvest you eat of tomorrow.

Train your ear to hear the Word of the Lord over the word of the world. Most of the time, the world offers no hope; it feeds on the negativity. God's Word not only offers hope but life and healing to your very bones. The Word of God will heal, fill, and restore what Satan has tried to steal, kill, and destroy. God's Word has power; as a Christian, your words have power.

The Word of God works when you work the Word. When you put the Word of God into your heart regularly, when times of need arrive, the Word will perfect and do what it was set out to do!

> Let the words of my mouth and the meditation of my heart be acceptable in Your sight, O LORD, my strength and my Redeemer.
> —PSALM 19:14

God's Word will never return void to those who believe, receive, and operate in God's love. Change your words and you will change your world; and give the devil something to fear!

28

LIVING IN THE CENTER OF GOD'S WILL, WILL PRODUCE GOD LIFE

Do not swerve to the right or the left; keep your foot from evil.

—PROVERBS 4:27, NIV

WHEN I SEE someone swerving in and out of lanes of traffic, I immediately go into defensive driving mode. Whether the person is in road rage, drunk, or just plain careless, I know he is dangerous. My daddy always taught us when we were learning to drive to stay behind someone like this; then you would know what he is up to. Satan, the enemy of your soul, needs to be kept in eyesight to know what he is doing.

When you know the will of God, you will know the enemy and his tactics. What about you? When you begin to swerve in and out of your spiritual life, are you aware of it? When you start to allow things that are of question to God's honor and you begin to swerve, are you aware? Are you accountable to others that speak into your life to get you back on track?

When you're accountable, you are teachable! The Holy Spirit desires to guide you into all truth before you fall. Satan desires to have God's children make wrong choices; this gives him a weapon to use against you throughout your day. Nevertheless, God has come to give you life and give it more abundantly. Find someone you can trust. Make yourself accountable to God first, then to a godly friend.

> Therefore confess your sins to each other and pray for each other so that you may be healed. The prayer of a righteous man is powerful and effective.
>
> —JAMES 5:16, NIV

In our world today, there are many distractions that can draw us away from the Word, to get us sidetracked from God's heart and will.

> Don't get sidetracked; keep your feet from following evil.
> —Proverbs 4:27, NLT

Keep your focus on the things of God. Temptation is appealing to the eye; in truth, the Bible tells us sin is pleasant for a season, but then judgment comes. God's heart (direction) for each of us is to be in the center of His will. Obedience aligns us with God's Word, which is His will for us.

> Finally, brothers, whatever is true, whatever is noble, whatever is right, whatever is pure, whatever is lovely, whatever is admirable—if anything is excellent or praiseworthy—think about such things.
> —Philippians 4:8, NIV

Be alert to your surroundings; be aware of the twisted truth that comes your way. Be accountable to God and man for who you are as a Christian. Focus on bringing God honor in each and every thing you do and say. This is where your life will produce His life for others to taste, touch, and see the love of God.

> Moreover, by them Your servant is warned; in keeping them there is great reward. Who can discern his errors? Acquit me of hidden faults. Also keep back Your servant from presumptuous sins; let them not rule over me; then I will be blameless, and I shall be acquitted of great transgression. Let the words of my mouth and the meditation of my heart be acceptable in Your sight, O Lord, my rock and my Redeemer.
> —Psalm 19:11–14, NASU

29

THERE ARE NO PLAIDS IN GOD: DETECTING THE GREY AREAS IN YOUR LIFE

> When the Spirit of truth comes, he will guide you into all the truth, for he will not speak on his own authority, but whatever he hears he will speak, and he will declare to you the things that are to come.
>
> —JOHN 16:13, ESV

WHEN FACING "GRAY areas," I don't ask, "What would Jesus do?" I ask, "What *did* Jesus do?" As Christians, we need to know what Jesus did when He was living on the earth. For if you know what He did, you will know what to do as you are facing untruths each day in your life experiences. The Word of God is what we are to use to guide our lives into all truth. We are to be the Christians of integrity of God's Word. Each person should cultivate integrity from and through the Word of God. Is your heart's desire to know the Word of God so you will do the will of God whether in gray, black, or white areas of life? There are no plaids in God!

For many years, because of my background of feeling rejected and unworthy, most all I did was for acceptance (approval) of man. I felt God was not happy with me. But through living for Him and seeing His grace unveiled to me as I studied His Word on a daily basis, I realized God loves and accepts me no matter how I feel. God promised me if I would do things His way, my feelings would catch up with His faith in me. Man can love you today and find you totally unacceptable tomorrow. God is not like this. My problem was that man's approval was my measure of how much God loved me; this led to many gray areas (plaid) resulting in decisions to please man rather than God.

It took some hard hits from men and women who changed the measure they wanted from me when I reached their goal. The hits were not all from horrible people—in fact, many were people of God—but I was looking for love and acceptance from man. Satan will use good people to hurt you, and they have no idea. Not all of them were at fault; the spirit of rejection was rooted in my childhood hurts and opened me to hurts as an adult. Fortunately, this took me to a place where I needed to go with God as Father rather than man as my ruler.

As I learned to accept God's forgiveness and love for me, I began exercising integrity. Truth and obedience please God. Living in His truth brings obedience and this led me to change my allowances in the gray areas. Never allow the spirit of rejection to hover over or direct your heart or life.

> But Peter and the other apostles answered and said: "We ought to obey God rather than men."
>
> —Acts 5:29

If you are trying to fulfill an image of the times or are setting your goals on what man says you should achieve, you will never be fulfilled. The images will change and what they expect will change; but God is the same today and forever. Every time you think you measured up to what they want, you will find their wants are different from what you thought their wants were!

God is nothing like man when you determine to honor Him and His Word. The Word of God says your gifts will make room for you. As you start on your journey of integrity, even if you fail, God will make it right as long as your heart is pure before Him. A desire to honor God cannot be man- or ministry-driven; it has to be God-called to fulfill His love on this earth.

God gave us a free will; we can choose to live in integrity or in a life of deceit. Deceit will catch up with you eventually. My mother said to always tell the truth and you won't have to make more lies when questioned. We are to live a life of truth. Jesus said in John 4:24, "They who worship Me must worship in spirit and in truth." When we live by and through the Spirit of God, the Holy Spirit, we will live a life of truth, which is a choice.

There are No Plaids in God

In today's world, there are choices we as Christians are confronted with. Just in case you need to know, there is no plaid in God; there is only black or white. When you mix the truth with darkness, you will get gray (plaid). When you take a white line and a black line and cross them you get plaid, and where the lines cross they produce gray. Do you have gray areas in your life?

Satan would use a question in Genesis, a twisted truth rooted in unfairness, to get woman to eat of the tree God had told her and Adam not to eat of. Taking truth then twisting it to your benefit is sin. When confronted with gray areas in your life, never let an unfair happening or past offense gray your judgment of truth. Always choose truth. Exercise truth; it will produce life.

> God is spirit, and those who worship Him must worship in spirit and truth.
> —JOHN 4:24

Is Christ your goal, is He the prize you are reaching for?

— 30 —

ARE YOU RUNNING THE RACE OR IS THE RACE RUNNING YOU?

> Friends, don't get me wrong: By no means do I count myself an expert in all of this, but I've got my eye on the goal, where God is beckoning us onward to Jesus. I'm off and running, and I'm not turning back.
> —Philippians 3:13–14, The Message

What controlled you yesterday will affect you today. Are you off and running the race God has set before you for this day? Are your plans His plans for your life today?

> A man's heart plans his way, but the Lord directs his steps.
> —Proverbs 16:9

There are times things happen in which you have no control; it seems all wrong, and at the time, there's no hope. But with God, all things can be turned around for His glory when we choose to allow His plan to take place.

> And we know that all things work together for good to those who love God, to those who are the called according to His purpose.
> —Romans 8:28

There are times in life when God's purpose and my plan collide. This is when I have to go back to the altar of God and find what He had in mind from the beginning. Not to say all my plans are bad—in fact, they can be good plans—but they are just not what the heart of God had in mind for me at the time.

Have you settled for good instead of great in God? God's Word says if you want to be great in God's kingdom, learn to be servant of all. Serving in God's kingdom is one of the most rewarding things a child of God can do. Many think service has to do with a platform or a large ministry. God says when we have done this to the least of these, we have done it unto Him. God is calling us to run with Him, to live like Him, to love like Him, and to follow His steps.

Moving forward in faith takes love, empowerment, and forgiveness. Running the race means looking forward in faith with love, believing I can reach the goal set before me. Live every day empowered by God in a greater measure than in myself. Creflo Dollar says, "If you can do it on your own, you don't need God." When something is bigger than you are, then only God can do it for or through you.

The test is not how strong you are or even how long the race is; the question is, will your faith endure until the end? Are you running the race with God or is the race running you? No matter the cost, will you continue to run, and not turn back?

> I press toward the goal for the prize of the upward call of God in Christ Jesus.
> —PHILIPPIANS 3:14

~ 31 ~

CAST ALL YOUR CARES ON HIM, WHO IS THE BURDEN BEARER

Casting all your care upon Him, for He cares for you.
—1 Peter 5:7

Roll them over before they roll over you! Too many times in our lives as Christians, we wait until we can't stand something in our lives any longer to give the problem over to God, to allow Him to help us with it. Why? Is it our nature as humans to hold on to the last moment to prove to God we can do this on our own? Is it pride that will not allow us to feel weak and undone, as if in asking God for help we have somehow failed? May we all come to a place of faith in God that we give everything in our lives over to Him!

Turn all your anxiety over to God because He cares for you.

> Darby Translation: "Having cast all your care upon him, for he cares about you."

> Weymouth New Testament: "Throw the whole of your anxiety upon Him, because He Himself cares for you."

> World English Bible: "Casting all your worries on him, because he cares for you."

According to AnxietyinAmerica.com, here are just a few reasons for anxiety in one's life today. There are numerous causes of anxiety that lead us to feel restless, stressed out or pressured, and being alone. In 2010, UCLA released their findings of more than two hundred thousand college students polled in the US. The finding shows that students are more stressed than ever in the history of our country and when asked about their fears, they said their biggest fear is what is going to happen.

Forty million US adults, or one in six adults, suffer from an anxiety disorder, and anxiety disorders are the most common mental illnesses in adults and children. The six anxiety disorders are generalized anxiety disorder, obsessive-compulsive disorder (OCD), post-traumatic stress disorder (PTSD), social anxiety disorder (social phobia), panic disorder, and specific phobias.

Jesus Christ came to take all disorders, fears, mental sickness, and anxiety away. He made a way for us to not have to carry these burdens. Cast all your cares, anxiety, disorders, pain, fear, and whatever it is that is keeping you from being all He created you to be—cast, throw, hurl, roll, put over onto Jesus and His cross so you may be free in Jesus' name.

As believers we are not to live as the world lives; God's ways are higher than our ways. He said He would make a way when there seems to be no way. God is a just God; He is one who will give you direction to come to greatness in Him as His child. He does not want any one of His children to live under the lie of the world; saying you have to be like this, you have a disorder. God sent His Son to the cross for your disorder. He paid the price for you to be free in spirit and in your soul (mind, will, and emotions).

There is nothing too big for your God. Cast all your cares upon Him, for He cares for you. Roll them over before they roll over you. Satan wants to destroy your life, your hope, and your joy, but God came to give you a greater day and future with hope. Live in the now and allow God to help you along the way to walk in freedom, for He is the burden bearer.

> For I know the thoughts that I think toward you, says the Lord, thoughts of peace and not of evil, to give you a future and a hope."
>
> —JEREMIAH 29:11, NKJV

⌒ 32 ⌒

FORGIVENESS—A POWERFUL FORCE!

> And David said to Saul: "Why do you listen to the words of men who say, 'Indeed David seeks your harm'? Look, this day your eyes have seen that the Lord delivered you today into my hand in the cave, and someone urged me to kill you. But my eye spared you, and I said, 'I will not stretch out my hand against my lord, for he is the Lord's anointed.'"
> —1 Samuel 24:9–10, NKJV

Decree and declare—if you will begin to speak into the atmosphere what God wants to do, there will be an explosion of faith as you pray, and it will surely come to pass.

> You will also declare a thing, And it will be established for you; So light will shine on your ways.
> —Job 22:28

Forgive -gave, -given, -giving. Verb (used with object)
1. To grant pardon for or remission of (an offense, debt, etc.); absolve.
2. To give up all claim on account of; remit (a debt, obligation, etc.).
3. To grant pardon to (a person).
4. To cease to feel resentment against: to forgive one's enemies.
5. To cancel an indebtedness or liability of: to forgive the interest owed on a loan.

Verb (used without object)
6. to pardon an offense or an offender

Forgiveness:
1. Act of forgiving; state of being forgiven.
2. The disposition of or willingness to forgive.

Pardon:
3. the act of forgiving or the state of being forgiven
4. willingness to forgive

Luke 12:48 says "Too much is given much is required"! When we have forgiveness shown to us, we are required by God to give the same forgiveness when we have been done wrong, betrayed and disappointed! The Golden Rule in Luke 6:31 says "do unto others as you would have them do unto you." How do you want to be treated in time of needing forgiveness, fairly, justly, righteously?

Do people deserve to be forgiven, most likely not; but do you? It seems we can internalize our wrongs to make it seem justified why we should be forgiven; because we are looking from the inside out! But when looking at others we have a different view, we view the situation from our pain not from the Father's Word. Truth is, through the blood, love, and cross of Jesus, everyone can have forgiveness. Now do we deserve forgiveness from God or anyone else? Most likely not, but it isn't about deserving forgiveness, it's about what God says about releasing others from the penalty of sin! When Jesus came into your heart to live He gave His only begotten Son Jesus that you and I can live in forgiveness without the pain of the past and guilt of our sins. This is why forgiveness is such a power, it truly is a powerful force in the life of all who will live and exercise it in their lives.

Forgiveness is never justified unless you do it! When David was anointed to be king he wasn't yet sitting in the office. He had to choose daily to forgive Saul. Every time Saul tried to take him out or even kill him, he had to choose to forgive! Sometimes it looked like David was weak; but he wasn't, he was strong in his trust in the Lord of his life. He chose not to retaliate but forgive. What a powerful force this act of forgiveness!

How do you make forgiveness a power force in your life?

1. You must do it; it is by an act of faith not feelings. When you choose to forgive, says you release the person from their act of pain against you.

2. You must continue to release forgiveness it may not be a one-time thing. It is always by faith, but you must choose to let the hurt

feeling go. Now it is your turn to release what has been said, what has been done and what you think about the situation over to God and allow Him to do His best ministry, heal your heart and mind.

> Jesus said to him, "I do not say to you, up to seven times, but up to seventy times seven."
> —Matthew 18:22, nkjv

3. You must trust God to do what He said he will do. Allow God to be the justifier, the vindicator, and most of all, the entire grace distributor. Ask God to give to the one who has hurt you the same healing you want for yourself.

4. Don't rehearse the pain of the sin. Don't allow your mind to go where you have already been healed by faith. Satan would love for you to replay the scenario over and over, but each time tell Satan, God is at work, He is the healer and there is no malice in your heart toward whomever hurt you (say their name) so you can be healed.

> Brethren, I do not count myself to have apprehended; but one thing I do, forgetting those things which are behind and reaching forward to those things which are ahead.
> —Phillipians 3:13, nkjv

5. Forgiveness becomes a powerful force when you do it first! Don't wait for God to tell you that you need to forgive. Anytime you have that feeling come on you that you were unjustly done, roll it over on to the cross of Calvary. Don't allow old pain to determine the destiny of your today.

Forgiveness is a powerful force. Release it today and see what God really wants to do in your life and in others.

> Don't pick on people, jump on their failures, criticize their faults—unless, of course, you want the same treatment. That critical spirit has a way of boomeranging. It's easy to see a smudge on your neighbor's face and be oblivious to the ugly sneer on your own. Do you have the nerve to say, "Let me wash your face for you," when your own face is distorted by contempt?
> —Matthew 7:1–4, msg

Forgiveness does not say you agree with the one who hurt you, it says you are free from the pain and bondage, and you are released to be the real you.

33

YOU CAN DEPEND ON GOD

For I am the Lord, I change not.

—Malachi 3:6, kjv

Do you really believe you can depend on God? Times change, you change, your looks change, your shape changes, your financial status changes, you're single, you're married, you're divorced, you're poor, you're rich; life is a series of changes. God says He changes not! If we are forever changing, then what can we learn from the text that says God changes not?

You can depend on God never to change His heart toward you, and He is never silent. Just because you can't hear God doesn't mean He is not there. Just because you are not hearing as clear as you want, that should not change your dependency on God. God is speaking throughout the world with and without the use of audible measures. His Word never returns void, and His life never ceases to give life to all who believe.

His breath is in every living creature. Many do not acknowledge Him. If you have Christ, you should be renewed by His love and power. Maybe you feel today that God has somehow failed you; maybe things did not turn out as you desired. God is faithful; look back even at the last hour of your life and see that He sustained you, He helped you, He kept you, and He provided for you.

Believer and unbeliever benefit from God being God! We know as believers because we have learned of the goodness of God, through good and bad times. In spite of our feelings, we know we can depend on Him deep down in our hearts, but what about in our heads? You can trust and depend on God!

When we start to think God has not been trustworthy, this is when we will start to feel abandoned, then rejected. We will start to think we are broken; then as a man thinks, he will become. The longer you dwell on what is wrong, the more wrong it will become.

Like King David, we may have bad times or circumstances that seem to be against us. But if you will allow the Holy Spirit to speak the Word of God to your heart, the Word within you will work. The Word works when you work the Word in you!

When you allow the Word to work on you, it will work in you! When you allow the Word of God to work on you, and in you, then He will work through you! You can depend on God; you can rely upon Him; He is trustworthy. He is faithful, He is consistent, and He is all-powerful on your behalf and others. Trust Him, love Him, and you will know, see, and understand, "You can depend on God."

34

LET GOD'S LOVE SHINE!

> Rejoice in the Lord always. Again I will say, rejoice! Let your gentleness be known to all men. The Lord is at hand.
> —PHILIPPIANS 4:4–5

IF EVER WE needed to be rejoicing in a time of trouble, it is now! Each new year, specialists forecast the year to be either the greatest or the worst. You and I as Christians do not live by the forecasts of specialists; we live by the Word of God. If there has ever been a time to live in faith, it is now. Many say we are to live by faith, but I say we *must* live in faith. Surround your life in faith with people who are faith-minded and those who look up when everything looks down.

> Now faith is the substance of things hoped for, the evidence of things not seen.
> —HEBREWS 11:1

Hope will not disappoint; hope brings a reason to rejoice before something materializes in the natural. We trust in the supernatural and put all our efforts into God, His Son, His Word, and the Holy Spirit. When the body of Christ becomes a joyous people no matter the circumstance, then the world will see we are Christians in good times and in bad.

> Let not your heart be troubled; you believe in God, believe also in Me.
> —JOHN 14:1

We have an assurance in God and His Word. His Word will not return void to all who believe! Will you let His love shine? Will you choose to rejoice in spite of what might seem to be the most

Let God's Love Shine!

difficult of times? Where have you placed your hope? Where is your strength coming from? Where is your trust, in God or man? Fear of man, fear of the future, fear of the past, fear of the "what ifs" will steal your joy for today and keep God's love from shining through you!

> For as he thinks in his heart, so is he.
> —PROVERBS 23:7

Whatever we think on is where we put value. If we ever needed the Word of God in our lives, it is now! Each day I challenge you to read your Word, put the Word in your mind, in your heart, in your being. John Maxwell says if you want to grow in the things of God, you must "read, learn, file." If you have placed the Word of God in your heart, then when Satan comes to try to steal, kill, and destroy, you will have the weapons you need to detect and annihilate him and his assignments against you. Satan is a liar; Jesus is the Author and Finisher of your faith.

Never give ownership of your faith away! No matter what you are facing, you are not facing it alone; you have God, His Son, Jesus Christ, and the Holy Spirit. Never allow the world's darkness to steal your light. You are the one God has chosen to shine through; will you be a dispenser of His love every day? When you give God permission to live and love through you, you can change your world!

> Let your light so shine before men, that they may see your good works and glorify your Father in heaven.
> —MATTHEW 5:16

35

PEACE IS YOURS TODAY; DON'T FORFEIT IT!

Don't forfeit your peace because of trouble and fear.

But the Counselor, the Holy Spirit, whom the Father will send in my name, will teach you all things and will remind you of everything I have said to you. Peace I leave with you; my peace I give you. I do not give to you as the world gives. Do not let your hearts be troubled and do not be afraid.
—JOHN 14:26–27, NIV

God's Peace Is:

Paid for by God through His Son, Jesus Christ. Peace is not an option with God, for His Son paid for it to be in your life. We have peace with God when we have peace in Jesus. He paid for everything! All sin, all rejection, all sickness, everything you face today, good or bad, God has the answer. Let His peace be the umpire of your life.

For he is our peace, who hath made both one, and hath broken down the middle wall of partition between us.
—EPHESIANS 2:14, KJV

Eternal. Man cannot give it to you. Fear will rob you of your peace; faith will build your spirit man to be all God called you to be. God has given peace through His Son, Jesus.

Peace I leave with you, My peace I give to you; not as the world gives do I give to you. Let not your heart be troubled, neither let it be afraid.
—JOHN 14:27

Abiding. When God sent His Son, it was to have fellowship with each one of His children. He is an abiding Savior. He is not only a God of peace; He created it!

> And I will pray the Father, and He will give you another Helper [*Parakletos*: an intercessor, consoler, advocate, comforter] that He may abide with you forever.
> —JOHN 14:16

Comforting. He is the God of comfort. No other god can bring you this peace. Buddha, Muhammad—they bring fear and discomfort. God is true peace. His Holy Spirit is the Comforter, and nothing can separate you from His love which produces peace.

> Do you think anyone is going to be able to drive a wedge between us and Christ's love for us? There is no way! Not trouble, not hard times, not hatred, not hunger, not homelessness, not bullying threats, not backstabbing, not even the worst sins listed in Scripture.
> —ROMANS 8:35, THE MESSAGE

Encourages us to go on. In spite of conflict, we can have peace. We have a sense God is with us. He is here to guide, to comfort, and to love through the best and the worst of times. For He is the God of peace.

> You will keep *him* in perfect peace, *whose* mind *is* stayed *on You,* because he trusts in You.
> —ISAIAH 26:3

In Greek, the meaning for *peace* is "to be at quietness, rest, or to set as one again." The Hebrew equivalent is Shalom, meaning "peace, completeness, and welfare." There may not be absence of war in your life right now, but your soul, mind, will, and emotions will not be moved as you put your trust in Jesus Christ. You will know whatever comes or goes, Christ is with you! He will direct your life for such a time as this; when you allow His peace to be the guide of your life, you can have assurance trouble or fear will not steal the peace of God.

No matter what is happening around you, God's peace is always there!

> Be anxious for nothing, but in everything by prayer and supplication, with thanksgiving, let your requests be made known to God.
> —PHILIPPIANS 4:6

36

WHAT HAVE YOU PUT ON THE SHELF?

> For as the rain comes down, and the snow from heaven,
> And do not return there, But water the earth, And make
> it bring forth and bud, That it may give seed to the sower
> And bread to the eater.
> —ISAIAH 55:10–11, NKJV

THE WORD OF God should not just sit there like a museum of antique truth that you can visit if you wish but otherwise avoid. Prophecy means a foretelling of future events—truth based on spiritual inspiration. In the past I have said and heard others say, if you receive a prophetic word, just put it on the shelf and if it comes to pass it is the Lord; if not, then you will know it was man. Yet we read in Hebrews, the Word is alive and powerful (Heb. 4:12).

> For the word of God is living and powerful, and sharper than any two-edged sword, piercing even to the division of soul and spirit, and of joints and marrow, and is a discerner of the thoughts and intents of the heart.
> —HEBREWS 4:12, NKJV

When God's truth is read, spoken, studied, preached, reflected upon, and obeyed, it changes individuals' lives. It alters relationships. It renews families. The Word of God transforms organizations, churches, businesses, even governments. There are many of you today, along with myself, that have had prophetic words spoken over and into our lives, yet we have allowed time to steal our joy of the words that were given. Spirit-directed words that brought such strength when they were being said. When they were spoken through the Word, the Holy Spirit, or a servant of God, we knew that we knew the truth was being downloaded into our souls.

It's time for the body of Christ to arise and take the words of life that were spoken into and over our lives and put them into actions and deeds. God is stirring the water for us to step into what He is doing for His glory in the world today. Yes, He is going to use you and me to do these great acts on His behalf. God ministers through people; He moves through His family; He operates for His glory through ordinary people to see His extraordinary miracles happen.

Don't let circumstances change what God has promised you; in fact, look at what is happening around you and know God is up to something awesome in your life. Satan is defeated; God is the author and finisher of your faith. When we look to God and trust Him to produce fruit when there seems to be no hope in sight, this is when God will be the Father He has promised to be to His children. We are given to by God, not based on good or bad merit, but by faithfulness to His Word, which says He will produce fruit and His Word will not return void for those who believe.

What have you put on the shelf that God has promised? Examine your life today and call those things to life God has said would live and not die! Prophecy will live in the one who believes and receives the power to go on no matter the situation, no matter the failure. When we trust God and walk in humility and repentance, He is faithful to keep and perform His Word in and through our lives for His kingdom's expansion.

> As it is written: "I have made you a father of many nations." He is our father in the sight of God, in whom he believed— the God who gives life to the dead and calls things that are not as though they were.
> —ROMANS 4:17, NIV

He who has begun a good work in you will complete it! Speak God's life over your life; speak the Word of God over the prophetic promises God has given you. Then you will see His destiny for your life come to be! Speak the Word, speak life!

> "For I am the Lord. I speak, and the word which I speak will come to pass; it will no more be postponed; for in your days, O rebellious house, I will say the word and perform

it," says the Lord God. Again the word of the Lord came to me, saying, "Son of man, look, the house of Israel is saying, The vision that he sees is for many days from now, and he prophesies of times far off. Therefore say to them, 'Thus says the Lord God: "None of My words will be postponed any more, but the word which I speak will be done," says the Lord God.'"

—Ezekiel 12:25–28, nkjv

37

HAVE YOU LEARNED TO LIVE IN CAPTIVITY?

Captivity comes from disobedience to God's Word.

That the LORD your God will bring you back from captivity, and have compassion on you, and gather you again from all the nations where the LORD your God has scattered you.
—DEUTERONOMY 30:3, NKJV

MANY CHRISTIANS TODAY have learned to live in captivity. The price of disobedience is captivity. Yet in our minds and with our mouths we say we are free, when all the while we know deep within there are many parts of our lives that are in captivity. We see repeatedly in the Word of God where the Israelites were on their way to the Promised Land only to end in captivity. Why? One word can answer this question: disobedience.

In our lives in Christ, there is only one thing that will keep us in captivity and this is disobedience. God is a God of truth; He is a God of love; and moreover, He is a God of goodness. He never wanted the Israelites to wander, to be in exile, or not reach the Promised Land. What He did want was obedience to His will, His Word, and His way. God has not changed today. He still wants us to live according to His Word, for in His Word there is life and freedom.

> By the rivers of Babylon, there we sat down, yea, we wept when we remembered Zion. We hung our harps upon the willows in the midst of it. For there those who carried us away captive asked of us a song, and those who plundered us requested mirth, saying, "Sing us one of the songs of Zion!" How shall we sing the LORD's song in a foreign land? If I forget you, O Jerusalem, let my right hand forget its skill! If I do not remember you, let my tongue cling to

the roof of my mouth—if I do not exalt Jerusalem above my chief joy.

—PSALM 137:1–6

Many times, like the Israelites, we don't know what we have until it is gone—not until we come to a hard place, far from our homeland, our God, and, yes, even people who are like us. This is when we can look back and see the goodness of God. We take for granted what is familiar because it is just that: familiar. God and His goodness, familiar, yes, and in many ways this can lead us into captivity.

As Christians, we should never take our relationship with God for granted. We should never let our lives become routine, calloused, or cold. God is a God of goodness and mercy and awe. He loves to direct our lives into joy, peace, and happiness. His intent was never for the Israelites to be in exile but fellowship and wholeness. These are His desires for you and me still today.

Will you sing today while there is still time to rejoice in God's goodness and mercy? Will you fill your heart with a song of deliverance in the midst of your tribulations? God never called His children to exile; He called us to a promise with an expected end and a hope. Captivity, many times, is self-induced, which gives Satan an open door to bring the children of God into spiritual and emotional bondage. The Word of God says Jesus learned obedience by the things that He suffered.

> Though He was a Son, *yet* He learned obedience by the things which He suffered.
>
> —HEBREWS 5:8

38

GOD SETS YOUR WORTH; YOU ARE THE APPLE OF HIS EYE

Keep me as the apple of the eye; hide me under the shadow of thy wings.
—PSALM 17:8, KJV

Apple of the eye: An English expression that refers to the pupil of the eye and therefore to something very precious. Three different Hebrew words or phrases are rendered as the apple of the eye: (1) the word in Deuteronomy 32:10 and Proverbs 7:2 literally means "little man" and evidently refers to the reflection of a person in the eye of another; (2) the word in Psalms 17:8 and Lamentations 2:18 (KJV) literally means "the daughter of the eye" with possibly the same significance as (1); and (3) the word in Zechariah 2:8 literally means "gate." In Lamentations 2:18 is to the pupil of the eye as the source of tears; the other references are metaphorical of something that is precious; Closeness or to be near.[1]

GOD SAYS YOUR worth is His Son going to the cross of Calvary for you! Everything you need is in salvation; not only eternal life, but every test, trial, or temptation and every triumph is paid for!

Do you have purpose? Are you drawn by God or driven by Satan? Maybe you have had so many things come at you, there seems to be no hope. God said, "My people perish for lack of knowledge" (Hosea 4:6). Are you being driven to make decisions you did not plan on? Are you at a crossroads where you have to do something, yet you don't know what to do? God is asking you not to be driven by choices, but to be drawn into His presence. There you will receive direction, which will produce His glory.

God Sets Your Worth; You Are the Apple of His Eye

Many times because we are not sure of who we are in Christ, we operate by emotions (feelings). This is when a person can be driven by fear of man, fear of not measuring up, or fear of failure. Fear is fueled by our wrong feelings; feelings are not to measure our worth in Christ. His Word is always our guidepost for living. Feelings will change, and they can fail, but faith will build up. Every living person on earth is valuable to God.

Think of someone you admire greatly in ministry. You are just as valuable to God! Only you can do what He has given you to do for His will to be accomplished on earth. All have sinned and fallen short of God's glory, yet God is asking you to get up, to rise above whatever Satan, man, or even self has brought your way! Will you be all He called you to be for the building of His kingdom?

Yes, you have a ministry, and yes, there is work to be done. And it really only can be done by you. Earthly positions or possessions do not measure value; transformation from the old life into the resurrected life makes one's life priceless in Christ.

You are the apple of His eye! He loves you, and He desires you to be drawn to Him, to be loved by Him, to be instructed, inspired, and cared for through His Spirit. You are to be a reflection of His life. You are precious to God, His Son, and His Holy Spirit! Everything you do should reflect the image of Christ. Satan drives us, but God draws by His love, mercy, and grace. In the middle of your test, trial, temptation, or even your triumph, don't doubt God's love for you. You are the apple of His eye.

> For thus says the LORD of hosts: "He sent Me after glory, to the nations which plunder you; for he who touches you touches the apple of His eye."
>
> —ZECHARIAH 2:8

39

IF MONEY CAN FIX IT, YOU DON'T HAVE A PROBLEM

For the love of money is a root of all kinds of evil. Some people, eager for money, have wandered from the faith and pierced themselves with many griefs.
—1 Timothy 6:10, niv

My daddy many years ago told me, "Sheila, if money can fix, repair, or restore something, you really don't have a problem." He said sooner or later the things you need will be provided for. Matthew 6:33 says, "Seek first the Kingdom of God and all these things will be added to you." My daddy had been hurt in an accident, which left him where no doctor could heal him. He knew only a miracle would give him back his health.

I went by to spend some time with my daddy and was telling him that with the two small children and Tim working for his father and not getting paid a lot, everything seemed due all at one time. Tim (my husband) and I needed tires for our car, which we could not afford at that time. There just wasn't money for them in our budget. It was then that Daddy said, "Sheila, if money can fix it, you really don't have a problem. God will provide."

To some, my daddy may not have been the pillar of the church or someone who claimed to be super spiritual, but I remember him reading the Bible and encyclopedia daily. He told all six of his children he didn't get to finish high school, but he knew he was smart, so each day he read. The amazing thing was he lived his life as a Christian without all the religious baggage. He fed the hungry, took in the homeless, gave jobs to the jobless, and loved without strings.

When money can't fix it, you have a choice—worry or trust? Worry takes away from your life, but trust will inspire you to believe beyond what you see! Money is not our problem, trust is. If money can fix it, you don't need God. If God is your source of life, then remember, He will never see the righteous forsaken or His seed out begging for bread.

> Rejoice in the Lord always. Again I will say, rejoice! Let your gentleness be known to all men. The Lord is at hand. Be anxious for nothing, but in everything by prayer and supplication, with thanksgiving, let your requests be made known to God; and the peace of God, which surpasses all understanding, will guard your hearts and minds through Christ Jesus.
> —PHILIPPIANS 4:4–7

In memory of Eddie L. Hamilton, my daddy
September 7, 1933–December 25, 1997

40

TRUSTING CHRIST BEFORE THE CRISIS

Your feelings will catch up to your faith when you place your trust (faith) totally in God.

The Lord is good, a stronghold in the day of trouble; and He knows those who trust in Him.
—Nahum 1:7

Before trouble comes, remember:

1. God is Good!
    Let's break Nahum 1:7 apart to see what God is really saying to Nahum in these terrible times. He tells Nahum in verse 7, "The Lord is good." No matter what is going wrong, no matter what is happening that appears to be the opposite of God's Word, He is good. All good and perfect gifts come from above. God can turn around your trouble for His glory. Never let your feelings rule you in times of trouble; let the Word of God be your guide and your strength.

2. God is your strong tower and your defense.
    The Word of God says in Nahum 1:7, "A stronghold in the day of trouble." Don't look around for a safe place anywhere else but in God. He is your stronghold and your defense. He is the place to be fortified in to stand against the wiles of the enemy when it seems you are losing your will to win. Your feelings will catch up to your faith if you place your trust in God. God is the Rock that will not be

shaken when everything around you seems to be falling apart. You can trust in God, the Rock of your salvation.

3. Trouble will come!

> In this you greatly rejoice, though now for a little while, if need be, you have been grieved by various trials.
> —1 Peter 1:6, NKJV
>
> We are told trouble is going to come, so be prepared to win, not lose. God did not call you to failure but to a future with hope and an expectant end for His glory. Trouble is an opportunity to triumph.

For I know the thoughts that I think toward you, says the Lord, thoughts of peace and not of evil, to give you a future and a hope. Then you will call upon Me and go to pray to Me, and I will listen to you.
—Jeremiah 29:11–12

When trouble, the adversary of this life, brings afflictions to your body or soul, or anguish to your spirit because of betrayal of a friend, you are to trust the Word of God for Him to be your defense. When tribulation seems to billow over you, never count yourself out when God is on your side.

Repent in the midst of the tribulation, things known, or things unknown, and you will see the power of God increase in your life, and His power will prevail when your trust is pure.

4. God knows those who trust Him.

> ...but speaking the truth in love, may grow up in all things into Him who is the head—Christ.
> —Ephesians 4:15, NKJV
>
> This word *trust* means "to flee to Him for protection." It means "to confide in; to have hope in; to take refuge, or to make refuge in"—literally, to put your trust in Him.

Selahs from God

> He is a double-minded man, unstable in all his ways.
> —James 1:8

If a double-minded man is unstable in all his ways, then a man or woman who has a single heart toward God can expect everything the Word of God says he or she can have. When trouble comes, you cannot afford to be double-minded. Be fixed, focused, and firm in your faith in God and His Word.

Many Christians are strangers to God until trouble comes, but God knows those who trust Him. We are told trouble is going to come. We are also told we will be triumphant when we place our trust in God and walk in obedience to Him. I ask you today, which way do you face life and what it brings? Do you know God, His Word, and His promises, or are you trying to get to know Him in the middle of your storm? Choose to know Him before the crisis comes; make a conscious choice to choose Christ, and then you will know what to do in the middle of your trouble. Trusting in God will never disappoint.

> For the Scripture says, "Whoever believes in him will not be disappointed."
> —Romans 10:11, NASU

~ 41 ~

DO I TRUST GOD, NO MATTER WHAT?

> Trusting God builds your faith; faith moves by the Word of God. Feelings are never to be your guide. Obey the voice of God and the Word of the Lord, and then your feelings will match your faith.

How do you know you are hearing God's voice? Feelings or faith? The Word of God is to be your guide in all you do, never your feelings. When what you hear aligns with the Word of God, as you study the Word of God, you will know His voice.

> Trust in the Lord with all your heart and lean not on your own understanding; in all your ways acknowledge him, and he will make your paths straight.
> —Proverbs 3:5–6, niv

> Trust in the Lord with all your heart; do not depend on your own understanding. Seek his will in all you do, and he will direct your paths.
> —Proverbs 3:5–6, nlt

What do you use for your life's compass, feelings or faith? Human feelings will fail. As believers, we must place our trust in God and His Word. The Word of God will build our faith to understand He knows all, and we will benefit when we place our trust in Him. When we truly trust God, we have to give our life over to Him, making sure we do not take it back! We need to trust Him, no matter what!

Real trust leaves life and its circumstance in God's hands in spite of what is going on or how we feel emotionally. Trust and confidence are developed when faith is exercised. The more we exercise our trust in God, the more our faith will grow. Each believer has been given a mustard seed of faith; now grow a tree, with fruit. No matter how insightful, wise, experienced, or knowledgeable someone may be, only God can guide the steps of a life properly.

> But you, beloved, building yourselves up on your most holy faith, praying in the Holy Spirit.
> —JUDE 1:20

Every believer needs to build his or her faith, no matter how mature; our faith is always being tested.

> A man's heart plans his way, but the Lord directs his steps
> —PROVERBS 16:9

We may think we know God's plan for our life, but Satan is out to thwart it whenever he can. Ask God to be the author and finisher of your life, and allow Him to direct your steps each day.

God asks us to trust Him and His wisdom even when we cannot immediately see the rationale behind it. God will take the ridiculous to do the miraculous, if we will allow Him to. He wants His children to recognize His presence, guidance, and grace in all we do.

Do you trust God with your entire life; do you rest in Him when everything seems to be spinning out of control? Satan wants God's children to feel and think God is not there, and sometimes it does feel like He isn't. As children of God, we have a covenant with the Father. He is always there, and He is always watching over you, so trust Him. As we trust and as we acknowledge His presence, we suddenly realize that our paths are a lot straighter and our destiny is so much closer.

> By your words I can see where I'm going; they throw a beam of light on my dark path.
> —PSALM 119:105, THE MESSAGE

~ 42 ~

TURN YOUR PAIN INTO MINISTRY—WILL YOU TRUST ME?

> And we know that all things work together for good to them that love God, to them who are the called according to *his* purpose.
>
> —ROMANS 8:28, KJV

TOMMY BARNETT OF First Assembly of God, Phoenix, Arizona, with more than ten thousand members, says "Turn your pain into ministry."

Whatever you are facing today can become something awesome in the hands of God if you will do it His way, for His glory. He may ask you today to let go of something dear to you. He may ask you to pick up something you did not want to deal with. Will He ask you to step out of your comfort zone to make a difference in someone else's life? All pain will become ministry when you obey the will of God. What are you waiting for?

> But now, thus says the LORD, who created you, O Jacob, and He who formed you, O Israel: "Fear not, for I have redeemed you; I have called you by your name; you are Mine. When you pass through the waters, I will be with you; and through the rivers, they shall not overflow you. When you walk through the fire, you shall not be burned, nor shall the flame scorch you."
>
> —ISAIAH 43:1–2

In our world, so many are facing what seems to be the toughest of tough times. When we look into the Scriptures, we will see that we are not alone. Everything we face today has been dealt with in the Holy Bible. There is nothing too impossible with God, and there is nothing too difficult for Him to solve when and if we put our trust in Him.

- *Trust*: a firm reliance on the integrity, ability, or character of a person or thing.

- *Custody-care*: something committed into the care of another; a charge.

> Let not mercy and truth forsake you; bind them around your neck, write them on the tablet of your heart, *and* so find favor and high esteem in the sight of God and man. Trust in the Lord with all your heart, and lean not on your own understanding.
> —Proverbs 3:3–5

Trust cannot be put into your own understanding. Things will get in the way of our trust in God if we allow them to. We must remember the words Isaiah gave: "when you walk through." The word to look at here is *through*. I love definitions, and Webster's says *through* is "from the beginning to the end; (to read a letter through); to the end; (to carry a matter through); to a favorable or successful conclusion."

So many times, we are hung up in the fire or in the storm. God may have allowed you to go through something, but He does not intend for you to stay there. His heart is for us to grow through whatever comes up in our lives, to see His glory, and for our trials to become ministry for others to know, taste, and see how wonderful God is to His children. When others see the goodness of God, they too will be led to God in a spirit of repentance.

> But now, God's Message, the God who made you in the first place, Jacob, the One who got you started, Israel: "Don't be afraid, I've redeemed you. I've called your name. You're mine. When you're in over your head, I'll be there with you. When you're in rough waters, you will not go down. When you're between a rock and a hard place, it won't be a dead end.
> —Isaiah 43:1–2, the message

Turn Your Pain into Ministry—Will You Trust Me?

- Redeemed—You are free; no sin, no debt.

- Called you by name—He knows you; He has called you into His destiny, and you have a ministry to do.

- You are Mine—He knows you; He called you by name; He knows right where you are, and He knows your need.

- I will be there—You are His; He knows right where you are. No matter what you facing, you do not have to face it alone.

- You're in the raging sea, in the fire, in between a rock and a hard place—He will carry you through for His glory. There is nothing too deep, too hot, too hard, or too difficult for God. He is with you!

Maybe you will be like the children of Israel and will see the waters rolled back as God makes a way when there seems to be no way. He will never leave nor forsake you when you put your trust in Him!

43

HOW TRUE ARE YOU TO YOUR RELATIONSHIP TO GOD?

> But he said to her, "You speak as one of the foolish women speaks. Shall we indeed accept good from God, and shall we not accept adversity?" In all this Job did not sin with his lips.
>
> —Job 2:10

I**N OUR WORLD** today, it seems everyone wants to blame someone else for his or her sin, addictions, and temptations; yet when you look at Job, he does not blame. In fact, he chooses not to give in to what I call the "blame game." Satan loves it when we start to charge others with the responsibility of our sins. The Word of God tells us not to be the accusers of the brethren. In our world today, it is always someone else's fault. I am guilty of this also. But the truth is, if we sin by choice and then blame it on someone else, we are not honest with ourselves and surely not with God.

> He who vindicates me is near. Who then will bring charges against me? Let us face each other! Who is my accuser? Let him confront me!
>
> —Isaiah 50:8, NIV

> Then I heard a loud voice saying in heaven, "Now salvation, and strength, and the kingdom of our God, and the power of His Christ have come, for the accuser of our brethren, who accused them before our God day and night, has been cast down.
>
> —Revelation 12:10

We can learn much from Job. How he lived in prosperity and in poverty were the same through faith. He trusted the God who provided in good and bad times. He allows God to be God in spite of his feelings.

- When tests come, whom do you blame?

When there is no test, we seem to be able to serve God with all of our heart. However, when trouble comes and things go crazy, will we and can we act like Job, continuing to serve and trust God no matter what is taken away? So, whom do we blame? Job did not blame anyone. Instead, he trusted his God. When his wife said, "You should curse God and die," he would not because he was a man of faith in good and bad times. Job loved God and asked God to show him whatever displeased Him. He did not go looking for someone to blame.

- When is the last time God and Satan discussed you?

Job had a relationship with God, but his relationship to God was not based on things, but on relation. Job served God out of a heart of faith; it was his faith that strengthened him when everything was taken away. God is still God in the middle of the test, but we have to make the choice before we go into the test to be faithful to the relationship no matter what the cost.

- Is there anything noteworthy in your life that would make you a threat to Satan?

Job, according to the Word of God, was called righteous in the Bible. Yet God allowed Job to go through challenges for His glory. God knew what was in Job, but God wanted Job to know what was in him. Maybe right now you are not perfect. We see in Job's story it's not about being noteworthy, but that anyone who loves God can be tested.

- How will you respond if God allows Satan to bring a challenge to your life?

Though He slay me, yet will I trust Him.

—Job 13:15

The way you go into a relationship is most likely the way you will maintain it. Whether in crisis or triumphs, your faith must always be in God and God alone. As long as we have Jesus, there is no reason to be concerned. Faith should increase in trouble. In times of trouble, what is your response? If you go into a relationship in faith you will maintain in faith.

- Will you stay true no matter what goes wrong in your life?

> But He knows the way that I take; when He has tested me, I shall come forth as gold.
> —JOB 23:10

Job never really knew the reason he was picked to go through what he went through. However, this we know: he stayed true to His God and looked for the best in the middle of the hard times. In spite of family, friends, life, and death, he stayed true!

- How sure is your faith when trouble or triumph comes?

I think all would say it is easy to trust God in the triumph, in the good times. What about the bad, like Job who never blamed God? He kept his faith, and he was faithful to His God. The Bible never says exactly why God allowed him to be tested. Job passed the test and was replenished at the end of the test. Even if you cannot understand, can you adjust your heart to know God is in control and say, "I will learn from what I am going through" and "No matter what I have or have not, I will choose God, for He is everything I need"?

> Even so we speak, not as pleasing men, but God who tests our hearts.
> —1 THESSALONIANS 2:4

God tests the heart, not to let Him know what you are made of, but for you to know what you are made of. What needs to be released or increased in your life for His glory?

~ 44 ~

PUT YOURSELF IN THEIR SHOES

Are we listening for the cries of the needy?

> For he has not ignored the suffering of the needy. He has not turned and walked away. He has listened to their cries for help.
>
> —Psalm 22:24, NLT

Before you judge someone based on their need, put yourself in their shoes. Years ago there was a TV detective show called *Dragnet*. When the two detectives went to a crime scene, they wanted "just the facts." When God speaks a word to help, He is not like this TV show. He is like a Father, taking care of the need and asking questions later. Many times He will not give you the facts, for this would cloud your heart with whether the person really is in need or not.

If you were in need right now and needed someone to help, how would you feel if they asked you to fill out a questionnaire to see if you were fit for help? I know in our systems in church or business, we desire to have everything done in excellence. However, can I ask you: when was the last time you really did something for someone not expecting one thing back from it? On the other hand, what about a time when you saw a need and did something about it because of true compassion?

> Judge not, that you be not judged. For with what judgment you judge, you will be judged; and with the measure you use, it will be measured back to you.
>
> —Matthew 7:1–2

Somehow, in the art of learning, growing, and finding our destiny along the way, it seems we have lost the real meaning of loving and serving Jesus.

> Then the lord of that servant was moved with compassion, and loosed him, and forgave him the debt.
> —MATTHEW 18:27, KJV

Nowhere in Scripture do I ever see Jesus ask someone in need, how did you end up here? How much money did you make? Or, Did someone just help you? No. When Jesus met people, He loved them, served them, met their needs, and then informed them how to live a life pleasing to the Father. He always took care of their natural need to bring them to a place of higher living for His glory. Put yourself in their shoes.

The Word of God says if you have the power to help someone in need, "Just do it!" My heart is not to see and know the need, but do nothing; it is to serve God, serve others, and let God deal with the real issues of their lives. The Word of God says it is the goodness of God that leads men to repentance. How will anyone ever know the goodness of God if you and I don't serve, love, and take care of those not capable of doing it for themselves? If it is within your sphere of influence to help, when God instructs, it is not your place to judge, it is your place to serve. God will take care of the rest.

Put yourself in their shoes. In your time of need, how have you been treated? How do you want to be treated? God is a lover of souls, and He takes care of each one. What is God asking you to do today to help someone in need, truly expecting nothing in return, but serving from a heart of gratitude? God will not ask you to do more than you can, but He may want to stretch you to the next level. Put yourself in their shoes!

> If anyone has material possessions and sees his brother in need but has no pity on him, how can the love of God be in him?
> —1 JOHN 3:17, NIV

45

DON'T FIGHT LIKE THE WORLD; FIGHT WITH THE WORD

> For though we walk in the flesh, we do not war according to the flesh. For the weapons of our warfare are not carnal but mighty in God for pulling down strongholds, casting down arguments and every high thing that exalts itself against the knowledge of God, bringing every thought into captivity to the obedience of Christ.
> —2 Corinthians 10:3–5

The Word of God says in Proverbs 23:7, "So a man thinks so he becomes." If we think like the world, we will operate in the world's system.

> And do not be conformed to this world, but be transformed by the renewing of your mind, that you may prove what is that good and acceptable and perfect will of God.
> —Romans 12:2

When we renew our minds daily, we will operate in God's system, and only then can we see His glory in all we do, even when we have to fight.

I realize from past attacks of Satan, he does not fight fair. I must also say, as Christians we do not always play or fight fair either. Many times without even knowing it, we have taken on the ways of the world in our decision-making, our prayers, and our life in general. As we renew our minds to the Word of God, we will see where the world's system has infiltrated our lives. This is when we must repent and ask God to change our minds, wills, and emotions to match His Word, will, and way.

In the Book of Mark, Jesus was driven into the wilderness by the Spirit. Jesus won the battle of the flesh through the Word simply by using the Word of God to defeat Satan, the enemy of His soul. No matter how great the temptation, Jesus allowed the Word of God to fight for Him. Our greatest weapon against Satan is, "It stands written"! God's Word is the most powerful weapon. When the pressure is on, get into the Word of God and let it minister to your soul and spirit. His Word will defend, fight, and win the battle for you. Whatever you put in your spirit man will be what comes out. Let me put it in southern terms: "When you work the Word in you, the Word will work for you."

Check your heart; see what you have been storing in it. Is the Word of God your priority? Is His presence your desire? Is His Spirit your companion in all you do and say? *Romans 3:23 says, "For all have sinned and fall short of the glory of God."* There is not one person who has not failed God as a Christian. However, do we continue to fail or do we pick ourselves up and say, "God, I have allowed the ways of the world to creep into my heart and I repent now Lord Jesus"? Ask Him to fill you with His love, Spirit, and hope so nothing will be allowed to come between you and Jesus.

> Your word I have hidden in my heart, that I might not sin against You! [*In the heat of battle, choose the Word.*] Blessed are You, O Lord! Teach me Your statutes! [*Be teachable. Jesus is the greatest teacher of all!*] With my lips I have declared All the judgments of Your mouth. [*There is power in the Word, so speak it!*] I have rejoiced in the way of Your testimonies, As much as in all riches. [*Praise your way out of trouble into triumph!*] I will meditate on Your precepts, And contemplate Your ways. [*Keep your mind stayed on the Word and His Spirit.*] I will delight myself in Your statutes; I will not forget Your word. [*Enjoy Jesus. Don't look for a battle; look for a victory.*] Deal bountifully with Your servant, That I may live and keep Your word. [*Conviction is powerful; it will defuse the enemy's power.*] Open my eyes, that I may see wondrous things from Your law. [*Be alert to divine moments in your life to bring God glory.*]
>
> —Psalm 119:11–18

~ 46 ~

AN EMPTY HEART IS A GOOD PLACE TO START!

> Keep your heart with all diligence, for out of it spring the issues of life.
> —Proverbs 4:23

As humans, God knew we were going to have issues in our life. He also knew we would try to fix them on our own. The only way to repair a broken heart is to give it over to Jesus completely, then allow God to search the deep things to bring them to light for His glory.

"Not by might nor by power, but by My Spirit," says the Lord.
—Zechariah 4:6, nasu

An empty heart is a good place to start. This is where you began your journey with Jesus the day you asked Him to come in to live in your heart. You asked Him to forgive you of all your sin and make your life new again in Him. From the beginning of your relation with Jesus Christ, He was looking for a heart He could fill with His love, goodness, and most of all His originality.

He doesn't desire patterns or habits which were taught or brought down by the DNA of your parents, your spouse, your past spouse, your boss, or even your own mind. God wants to give you and me life, and give it more abundantly! To do this, He needs an empty heart!

Satan comes to steal kill and destroy but God came to give life and give it more abundantly (John 10:10).

God does not want our works but our servanthood; God doesn't want our funds, but faithfulness. God doesn't want our loot but His fruit developing in us. He wants our heart with nothing but Him in it, and then He can do in us what we have always thought but have been afraid to believe—and if we are afraid to believe, we will never receive.

> Cast all your cares on Him for He cares for you.
> —1 Peter 5:7

Many may feel they have not been cared for by God or man. This is why issues arise in our hearts. The truth about God is, He has been taking care of us in many ways that we cannot see. Unfortunately, many things that are in our hearts may have kept us from seeing all the goodness God has been doing in our lives.

As Christians, we need to totally empty our heart before God and release the issues that are in it. Then, allowing God to direct every area of our lives, we will see our lives align with His Word, will, and way. It may not be an instant fix, but it will be an ends to a means that will free us from oppression, pain, and suffering, which Christ already paid for on the cross of Calvary. Today we can choose to live under the curse of yesterday's sin or we can live in the resurrection power of the Lord Jesus Christ. Which one do you want? Do you want to stay like you are, or do you want to empty your heart to receive a fresh new start, giving all good and bad, which keeps you from the presence and fullness of God? It is your choice!

> Hope deferred makes the heart sick, but when the desire comes, it is a tree of life.
> —Proverbs 13:12

God desires to fill you with His presence, love, grace, and mercy every moment of your life. Not just sometimes but all the time! He does not want you just to come to Him when you have a problem, but He wants you to be in communion with Him twenty-four hours a day, seven days a week. He wants your heart—all of it. Not parts of it, but all of it!

In the authentic life in Christ, you have to make a choice daily to cast your cares on Him, to allow God and His Word to lead your life in the path in which He sees best. Each one of us will have issues in

An Empty Heart Is a Good Place to Start!

our hearts. We have to make a choice to cast (throw, hurl, roll) the issues over onto God. Or we can continue to hold on, thinking we can do this in our own strength.

This is exactly how we got in many of the things we are in, is because we did it our way instead of God's. Frank Sinatra's song "My Way" is too many Christians' silent theme song. We don't serve a Burger King God; we can't just have it our way. We are to live according to the Word of God, and when we do, we desire to live life His way.

If you need a fresh start, you must empty your heart. Obey today what the Lord has given you, and you will receive a new heart. An empty heart is one which has cast *all* its cares on the Lord and then trusts Him to finish what He has begun, obeying His direction on a moment by moment basis.

47

TIME ALWAYS TELLS THE TRUTH!

> For nothing is secret that will not be revealed, nor anything hidden that will not be known and come to light.
>
> —Luke 8:17

A secular song by Earth, Wind & Fire says, "Time is on your side." There is a freedom that comes when you realize time always filters out the schemes of Satan. Then as you place your trust in God, His peace will fill your heart and you will be willing to wait for God and His justice. This is when you can be glad that time is in God's hands!

Even if you feel like the world has turned against you and you seem to have lost everything, you can be assured truth is on your side. When you know the truth but you feel you're the only one who seems to see it, when all your friends, family, and others have moved on, even sided with, for a lesser word, "the enemy," you place your trust in the truth and wait!

> But those who wait on the Lord shall renew *their* strength; they shall mount up with wings like eagles, they shall run and not be weary, they shall walk and not faint.
>
> —Isaiah 40:31

I know that in the Word of God, it reveals truth in His time. When your life desire is to be a seeker of truth, and you trust, God is on your side! Time always tells the truth! His truth always brings freedom, not just to the one done wrong, but to all concerned when God is allowed to be God!

> So if the Son sets you free, you are free through and through.
>
> —John 8:36, the message

Time Always Tells the Truth!

When one is truly free and does not hold on to the past, it opens the heart to the will of God on a moment-by-moment basis. Truth should never be desired for the sake of being right, but for the righteousness of God to be seen by all involved. Just because you're right doesn't make you righteous.

> Wise Man Quote: "In life you will find there are normally three sides to a story: his, hers, and the most important—the truth!" (Tim Zellers)

No matter how fast or slow time may seem to move, freedom isn't about being right! It is about seeking the truth-giver, Jesus Christ, for His truth will set you free. No matter what pain you have suffered, allow God to heal you, then free you from it in all areas of your life.

How truly wonderful it is to be free in Christ. There is really nothing like it!

Remember, time is not on your side, but truth is. Life is but a vapor, so use your time wisely! Your life will show what and who you are, for God designed it that way; with this in mind, live truthful! Time will always tell the truth!

> Whereas you do not know what *will happen* tomorrow. For what *is* your life? It is even a vapor that appears for a little time and then vanishes away.
>
> —JAMES 4:14

— 48 —

TRUST IS PRODUCED IN GOD'S PRESENCE

Where you spend your time tells where you put your trust!

> But *it is* good for me to draw near to God; I have put my trust in the Lord God, that I may declare all Your works.
> —PSALM 73:28, NKJV

MANY TIMES IN our lives, people ask us to trust them. In business, in church, in work, we see infomercials that tell us this will change our life, just try it. Yet they do not tell the whole story, which says we have to put something in it to get something out. God desires us to spend time in His presence; this is where we will find God's perfect will for life!

Time is very valuable, and where you spend it tells what you value. It also shows where you put your trust. Who do you trust in more, man or God?

> Trust in the LORD, and do good; so shalt thou dwell in the land, and verily thou shalt be fed.
> —PSALM 37:3, KJV

Life is not always fair, but you can count on God to be! He is faithful; He will not betray your trust. Not only can you count on Him, but He also rewards obedience. There is a blessing in trusting Him.

We are to delight in God's presence; this is where you will find fullness of joy. Where is your delight today?

> Not that I speak in respect of want: for I have learned, in whatsoever state I am, therewith to be content.
> —PHILIPPIANS 4:11, KJV

Delighting in God's presence should not hinge on your feelings or your circumstances. Your feelings come and go, good and bad, but delighting in the Lord means you are choosing a lifestyle of being with Him. Being in His presence says you are choosing to trust Him in all things. In His presence is where you will be strengthened to be more like Jesus and where your trust will be increased.

> *Delight*: Great pleasure; joy. Something that gives great pleasure or enjoyment. To take great pleasure or joy: To give great pleasure or joy.[1]

Delighting in God is a choice! One must take time to take pleasure in God! This is a key to life, and we need to choose to take time in God's presence. His comfort will direct our lives to be more like Him daily. Being with Him should not be a chore but a choice!

> Delight thyself also in the LORD; and he shall give thee the desires of thine heart.
> —PSALM 37:4, KJV

No matter what you may be wanting from God—peace, health, hope—there seems to be a waiting period. God's presence is not limited by earthly time or by needs. He is there no matter when you call; His presence will comfort you.

> For the joy of the LORD is your strength.
> —NEHEMIAH 8:10, KJV

Oftentimes we get so involved with so many things. They are not all bad; they can be good things. Ministry, family, job, home—the list is endless. Doing too many things will weaken your commitment to not only God but to others also. As we place God at the top of our priority list, we will see many things fall into place that we never thought possible.

Jesus—His cross, His Spirit, His Word—must be priority one!

> Commit thy way unto the LORD; trust also in him; and he shall bring it to pass.
> —PSALM 37:5, KJV

> Commit to the Lord whatever you do, and your plans will
> succeed.
> —PROVERBS 16:3, NIV

> Commit your works to the LORD, and your thoughts will
> be established.
> —PROVERBS 16:3

> Therefore He is also able to save to the uttermost those who
> come to God through Him, since He always lives to make
> intercession for them.
> —HEBREWS 7:25

Jesus is not praying you will fail; He is praying for you to succeed! He desires you to be in His presence and His Word. True rest does not come from outside in, but inside out! Spending time in God's presence produces peace no man can steal.

Where there is no rest, there is no peace. Absence of peace will create a place for anger to grow. Anger is fear turned inside out. When the enemy of our life tries to get us to walk opposite of God's will, Word, and way, you need to stop, drop, and pray.

> Therefore submit to God. Resist the devil and he will flee
> from you.
> —JAMES 4:7

Trust God, submit to His will, resist by the Word, and you will see God's comfort, peace, rest, and most of all victory in your life.

> Rest in the LORD, and wait patiently for Him; do not fret
> because of him who prospers in his way, because of the
> man who brings wicked schemes to pass. Cease from
> anger, and forsake wrath; do not fret—it only causes harm.
> —PSALM 37:7–8

God's plan for your life comes from spending time in His presence—not only listening to His Word and voice, but also obeying the instructions He gives to you. God will give you the plan He has for your life

Trust Is Produced in God's Presence

as you spend more time in His presence, for this is where you will find His fullness and joy, and once again fall in love with Him all over again!

Trust and delight in Him! Commit all things to Him. Rest in Him, for true life comes from spending time in His presence.

49

PRAYING FOR YOUR SPOUSE

> For the unbelieving husband is sanctified by the wife, and the unbelieving wife is sanctified by the husband.
> —1 Corinthians 7:14, NKJV

I WAS BORN AGAIN into the family of God on January 24, 1984. I was born into the family of God the first time when I was four years of age, then baptized in the Holy Spirit when I was thirteen. As a young woman, I attended church and loved God with my whole heart. I met my husband at work when I was seventeen. We married November 19, 1977. Tim had gone to church with me, even though he had never been brought up in church at all. After we married, we slowly drifted away from the church and then away from God. It took an encounter with the world where I was given a choice to live for God or lose my marriage, children, and possibly my life. Thank God I chose Jesus!

That January night, God arrested me in my hotel room and showed me in advance the choices I would make and how it would end up. I am grateful for a praying mother who never stopped believing all six of her children would become children of God. I made a choice that night to follow God. I thought I would go home and Tim would just come along with me as he had when we were teens. He didn't; it took over thirteen years; but God instructed me that wonderful January evening how to pray, not just once but for years on a daily basis. God was faithful, and through it He taught me to be patient and to trust Him to complete what He promised.

If you are living with a spouse who is not yet a believer, I encourage you to pray this prayer over them; then allow God to speak to you about what you can do to help your spouse desire the love of God. For it will be the love of God that draws men to repentance. Treat them like they are a Christian, ask questions of the Bible, and love them as if they were already in the family of Christ.

It is called faith! Remember the unbelieving spouse is sanctified by the believing spouse! Keep praying and loving with unconditional love. Having a saved spouse is not about having a perfect family; it is about being one in God for His glory. May the prayer God gave me to pray for my husband help you as you pray for your spouse; whether they are saved—or not—the prayer is powerful!

> (Your spouse's name) *is a Mighty Man of God. He is taught and obedient to the Word. He hears the voice of the Good Shepherd, and that of a stranger* (Your spouse's name) *will not follow. He is rooted, grounded, and established in the Word of God. He is the high priest of our home, a man not of double purpose but stable and trustworthy in all his ways. Our family is united in the bond of love with peaceable communication to build and edify each member. No weapon formed against us will prosper in the name of Jesus. Amen.*

SPOUSE'S PRAYER CONTINUED: THE WORD OF GOD SAYS...

And they helped David against the band of the rovers: for they were all mighty men of valour, and were captains in the host.
—1 CHRONICLES 12:21

And all thy children shall be taught of the Lord; and great shall be the peace of thy children.
—ISAIAH 54:13

And when he putteth forth his own sheep, he goeth before them, and the sheep follow him: for they know his voice. 5And a stranger will they not follow, but will flee from him: for they know not the voice of strangers.
—JOHN 10:4–5

Rooted and built up in him, and established in the faith, as ye have been taught, abounding therein with thanksgiving.
—COLOSSIANS 2:7

But ye are a chosen generation, a royal priesthood, an holy nation, a peculiar people; that ye should shew forth the praises of him who hath called you out of darkness into his marvelous light:

—1 Peter 2:9

But let him ask in faith, with no doubting, for he who doubts is like a wave of the sea driven and tossed by the wind. For let not that man suppose that he will receive anything from the Lord; *he is* a double-minded man, unstable in all his ways.

—James 1:6-8, NKJV

That their hearts might be comforted, being knit together in love, and unto all riches of the full assurance of understanding, to the acknowledgement of the mystery of God, and of the Father, and of Christ;

—Colossians 2:2

For kings, and for all that are in authority; that we may lead a quiet and peaceable life in all godliness and honesty.

—1 Timothy 2:2

Wherefore comfort yourselves together, and edify one another, even as also ye do.

—1 Thessalonians 5:11

No weapon that is formed against thee shall prosper; and every tongue that shall rise against thee in judgment thou shalt condemn. This is the heritage of the servants of the Lord, and their righteousness is of me, saith the Lord.

—Isaiah 54:17

Blessed is the man that walketh not in the counsel of the ungodly, nor standeth in the way of sinners, nor sitteth in the seat of the scornful. But his delight is in the law of the Lord; and in his law doth he meditate day and night. And he shall be like a tree planted by the rivers of water, that bringeth forth his fruit in his season; his leaf also shall not wither; and whatsoever he doeth shall prosper.

—Psalm 1:1–3

~ 50 ~

GOD'S EXTREME MAKEOVER: ALLOWING GOD TO TRANSFORM YOU

> Don't become so well-adjusted to your culture that you fit into it without even thinking. Instead, fix your attention on God. You'll be changed from the inside out. Readily recognize what he wants from you, and quickly respond to it. Unlike the culture around you, always dragging you down to its level of immaturity, God brings the best out of you, develops well-formed maturity in you.
> —ROMANS 12:2, THE MESSAGE

How many of *you have ever tried to make yourself over… only to fail?* It seems no matter how hard you and I have tried to do better, be better, live better, within just a few days, maybe hours, we have failed. Why? Because we were trying to do it in our own power and our own strength. Anytime I do something in my own power, it will fail. I will fail me!

But when we offer ourselves as a living sacrifice, we are trusting God to do the work on us, in us, and then through us. *Each day, we make a choice to live our lives according to God and His way, joining Him in what He is doing.* We will see daily an extreme makeover in God and His goodness. *His extreme makeover happens as we learn to give ownership over to God, and yes, we do have a crucial role to play.*

We must choose to say no to the ways of the fallen world—or should I say the fallen flesh?—and say yes to the things of God. But that's not the whole story. *You will be able to discern and do God's will only when you "let God transform you into a new creation as you are changing the way you think." The original Greek calls us to "be transformed," not by our own efforts, but by the power of God.*

> For as he thinks in his heart, so *is* he.
> —PROVERBS 23:7

More love, more power. Oh, did I tell you? You don't have to fix this; you're not the Savior. You're the child of the Most High God. He paid the price for your extreme makeover through His Son.

> Set your mind on things above, not on things on the earth.
> —COLOSSIANS 3:2

The verb meaning, "be transformed" utilizes a Greek mood that conveys an ongoing process. Transformation is a process; do not skip the steps God is calling you to. Transformation doesn't happen automatically, once-and-for-all, when we first put our faith in Christ.

Rather, it is a lifelong process of opening ourselves to God's renewing power. Once you ask God to transform you, to do an extreme makeover, your will begins to fight God's will. This is when the process has to start over again and again, until the Spirit of God in you wins!

> I beseech you therefore, brethren, by the mercies of God, that you present your bodies a living sacrifice, holy, acceptable to God, *which is* your reasonable service. And do not be conformed to this world, but be transformed by the renewing of your mind, that you may prove what *is* that good and acceptable and perfect will of God.
> —ROMANS 12:1–2

God's transformation, His extreme makeover, is not an outward change but an inward one. It begins by the way of "changing the way you think." The renewed mind comes as you allow God's Word to teach you God's truth.

> But let him ask in faith, with no doubting, for he who doubts is like a wave of the sea driven and tossed by the wind. For let not that man suppose that he will receive anything from the Lord; he is a double-minded man, unstable in all his ways.
> —JAMES 1:6–8

If a double-minded man can expect nothing from God, a single focused man can expect God to do everything He promised when we operate in true faith.

When you meditate upon the Bible, using it as the basis for your daily prayers. Prayer is daily communication and prayer with the Father God. A new mind comes when you spend time with God and with other believers to study the Word, to hear it proclaimed and to experience it in the sacraments. Though we cannot transform ourselves, we can participate in that which opens our minds to the Spirit. As this happens, we will be able to know God's will so that we might not only desire it, but do it.

Nike did not invent "Just Do It"—God did!

Can I ask you? How eager are you for change? How extreme are you willing to be for God to make you over? Are you tired of living life the way it has always been and expecting a different result? How much of you are you willing to give up to get all of God?

God's Extreme Makeover: God paid the price, and now I can make the choice to follow Him; from the inside out!

51

WHERE YOU COMPARE, YOU WILL COMPETE!

> We do not dare to classify or compare ourselves with some who commend themselves. When they measure themselves by themselves and compare themselves with themselves, they are not wise.
>
> —2 CORINTHIANS 10:12, NIV

IN THIS LIFE, each of us will have an opportunity to be better or less, richer or poorer, fatter or skinnier than others. This is what makes life more interesting in many ways, doing something better than the next person, business, athletics, church, service. In the body of Christ, we are told to mourn when one mourns, laugh when one laughs, and cheer when one does greater than we do. It just seems to go against the grain of human nature. However, in Christ, we live by His Word, not man's control.

From the very beginning of our lives, each human is born into the world the same, yet each household is different. We are all humans, yet all fearfully and wonderfully made by God and His great creation. The United States Constitution says we are all created equal, yet there are rich, middle class, and poor. When you become a Christian, your family and social or economic status does not change; your heart does. You will live in the same house, maybe have the same job, and did I mention you still have the same family?

Where you compare, you will compete. God never called you and me to be saved to be compared to anything or anyone. We are to compete for one thing: the prize of the high calling in Christ Jesus. He called us to be complete in Him and His Word for our lives, each Christian to know Him and His love, grace, and mercy, to instill in others that they too can be all Christ called them to be!

Where You Compare, You Will Compete!

I press toward the goal for the prize of the upward call of God in Christ Jesus.

—Philippians 3:14

In this hustle and bustle world, sometimes as Christians we are no different from the world; we just package our competitiveness differently. In Proverbs 27:17, the Word of God says, "Iron sharpens iron." This is not to be a bad thing; it could be someone who has gifting greater than you challenging you to come up higher and then helping you do it. Where you compare, you will compete; it is human nature to do so.

There will always be someone smarter, richer, poorer, prettier, or sharper. If you measure up in your comparison, you risk being prideful. If you do not, then you risk feeling inadequate. Christ in you, the hope of glory, desires you to be all He created you to be. He called you into His family to fulfill you and develop the gifts and callings He placed in you before you were placed in your mother's womb. God loves you so much. He desires you to be what and who He created and planned for you to be.

When you compare yourself to others in a positive way, it will inspire you to grow in the natural and supernatural. When you look at yourself in a negative way, you will feel as if you will never make it, you will never measure up, and there is no hope for you. This is so far from God's truth. He has called you, and He knew you before you became flesh. He designed you from His original design to be great in His kingdom. Where you compare, you will compete. Desire the good gifts, and allow God to make you who and what He planned from the beginning of time for you to be: His! Completely His!

~ 52 ~

THE POWER OF YOUR WORDS

> Then God said, "Let there be light"; and there was light.
> —GENESIS 1:3

WORDS ARE POWERFUL and can be a weapon; they can build well or bad. Which are you building? When you speak godly words, then your life will become better in the future!

Our attitude is a reflection of our soul, which is defined as the mind, will, and emotions. Your words are an example of what is in your heart. Words have formed in our minds how we feel about ourselves and others. Words are powerful in your life, especially the words you not only say, but you think. Humans love affirmations about themselves, but many times we are the last ones to speak affirming words about ourselves or even accept them from others.

> And since we have the same spirit of faith, according to what is written, "I believed and therefore I spoke," we also believe and therefore speak.
> —2 CORINTHIANS 4:13

Through salvation we have faith—so we need to speak faith-filled words. "God words" bring power into our lives. Faith believes, and then your actions will confirm whom you have trusted in. "Faith words" establish God's life in you to destroy Satan's lies! God desires we release our faith by the words of our confession. Faith is not faith until it is activated!

What we believe will produce what we receive! Hebrews 11:2 says "Faith will obtain what God has promised!" Faith words produce life and prosperity; spirit, soul, and body.

For He spoke, and it was done; He commanded, and it stood fast. Speaking the word is the power to create God Life! What we say will reflect what we truly believe!

—Sheila Zellers

What you speak is what rules your heart. So a man speaks, so he thinks! My husband, Tim, says "a thought is a thing you think before you do." The Bible says, "For as he thinks in his heart, so is he" (Prov. 23:7). As God touches your heart, then your speech will change and your words will reveal your heart.

Pressure will reveal what is in your heart; also, God says in Luke 6:45, "Out of the abundance of the heart his mouth speaks. Test and trials reveal where your faith is. As you speak God's Word, your heart (mind, will, and emotions) is renewed and changed into Christlikeness.

God spoke, and all living things were made and continue on, even today. When you and I agree with God and His Word, our lives will align with His life to see the glory of God displayed in the earth today. Speak the Word of God everywhere you go. God is a life-giving God; He loves to hear you speak His Word over every area of your life to see His kingdom come and His will done here on earth.

Your words have power. You may not change the entire world, but you can change yours by speaking God's Word over your world. Make a difference, and know your words have power.

─ 53 ─

DEFEATING FEAR AND DOUBT
Faith repels the devil; fear empowers him.

> Knowing that the testing of your faith produces patience. But let patience have its perfect work, that you may be perfect and complete, lacking nothing. If any of you lacks wisdom, let him ask of God, who gives to all liberally and without reproach, and it will be given to him. But let him ask in faith, with no doubting, for he who doubts is like a wave of the sea driven and tossed by the wind. For let not that man suppose that he will receive anything from the Lord; he is a double-minded man, unstable in all his ways.
> —JAMES 1:3–8

Have you ever answered "I doubt it" to a question? Everyone at one time or another has had doubts and fears. Healthy fear is a fear of God. The fear of God is placed in you to protect you. The true question is: what fear are you operating in?

Do your doubts defeat you, or do you defeat them? Do your doubts stop you from doing what you could do if you didn't have them, or do you stare doubt in the face, tell it to move, and go on with your life? You have to speak to unhealthy fear. You must tell it to go back where it came from: Satan and his hell!

Think about that. What do you do when doubt and unbelief come to your mind? If you allow unhealthy thinking in, when you let doubts creep in, you're not going reach your full potential God created you for.

> If you do well, will you not be accepted? And if you do not do well, sin lies at the door. And its desire is for you, but you should rule over it.
> —GENESIS 4:7

Where does doubt come from? Where does fear come from?

> There is no fear in love; but perfect love casts out fear, because fear involves torment. But he who fears has not been made perfect in love.
>
> —1 John 4:18

> And above all things have fervent love for one another, for "love will cover a multitude of sins."
>
> —1 Peter 4:8

The Holy Spirit revealed to me that we are not sure of His love and that when we are uncertain of a thing, then we will doubt or distrust the validity of it. God has not called us to a spirit of fear, but to love and a sound mind. We are to have single mindedness in Him.

> For God has not given us a spirit of fear, but of power and of love and of a sound mind.
>
> —2 Timothy 1:7

When a believer knows without any doubt he or she is loved by God, forgiven, and most of all accepted, then his or her life will begin to stabilize for God's glory.

─ 54 ─

A DOUBTER'S TRAITS

The doubter is unstable.

If any of you lacks wisdom, let him ask of God, who gives to all liberally and without reproach, and it will be given to him.

—JAMES 1:5, NKJV

UNSTABLE MEANS "TO be not stable; not firm or firmly fixed; unsteady."

If there's one thing in life that everybody wants, it's stability. People want to know that they can go to work tomorrow and not worry about losing their job. They want to be able to stand on the ground beneath them and not fall through. Humans like routine. Routine in many lives equals stability. When something is unstable, it is easily swayed one way or another.

If you are unstable, you can be manipulated very easily. You'll believe everything that everybody says. You'll be gullible. The one definition for double-minded man is "a person drawn in two opposite directions." Because of his lack of sincerity, he sways between belief and disbelief, sometimes thinking that God will help him and at other times giving up all hope in Him.

DOUBTERS DON'T DO THE MIRACULOUS

Now in the fourth watch of the night Jesus went to them, walking on the sea. And when the disciples saw Him walking on the sea, they were troubled, saying, "It is a ghost!" And they cried out for fear. But immediately Jesus spoke to them, saying, "Be of good cheer! It is I; do not be afraid." And Peter answered Him and said, "Lord, if it is You, command me to come to You on the water." So He said, "Come." And when Peter had come down out of the boat, he walked on the water to go to Jesus. But when

he saw that the wind *was* boisterous, he was afraid; and beginning to sink he cried out, saying, "Lord, save me!"
—MATTHEW 14:25–30

Peter walked on water, but not for long. Jesus equated Peter's fear with doubt. So, he couldn't continue to walk on water or do the miraculous because he doubted. He looked at the wind and thought, "The wind's too much. I can't make it out to Jesus now. What am I going to do?" Peter couldn't do the miraculous when he doubted. At first, he wasn't afraid, he didn't doubt, and he started off walking on the water, but when he felt the wind, things changed. How about you? Have you ever started something with full force, only to be faced with certain challenges that cause you to doubt and give up?

Is there something God has asked you to do and you had all the good intentions to do it but fear held you back? Did something someone said discourage you from stepping out? Did you allow fear and doubt to limit what God wanted for you? That's the only way you'll be where God wants you to be. Sometimes life is like a stormy sea and sometimes you have to get out of the boat and walk on water to get to where you want to go.

DOUBTERS DON'T PLEASE GOD

> But without faith it is impossible to please Him, for he who comes to God must believe that He is, and that He is a rewarder of those who diligently seek Him.
> —HEBREWS 11:6

The doubter cannot please God because doubt signifies a lack of faith, and according to the Scripture, faith is a requirement to please God. I want to make God smile; I want to be a God-pleaser rather than man. I'm determined to defeat the doubt that comes my way.

Four ways to overcome fear and doubt:

1. *Replace fear with faith in God. Change your mind, change your faith.* "So Jesus answered and said to them, "Assuredly, I say to you, if you have faith and

do not doubt, you will not only do what was done to the fig tree, but also if you say to this mountain, 'Be removed and be cast into the sea,' it will be done" (Matt. 21:21).

2. *Know God's Word and stand firm on it. God's Word has the power to create a new you from the inside out!* "That He may incline our hearts to Himself, to walk in all His ways, and to keep His commandments and His statutes and His judgments, which He commanded our fathers" (1 Kings 8:58).

3. *Ask God for wisdom. Obey the instruction God gives—His wisdom will not fail.* "If any of you lacks wisdom, let him ask of God, who gives to all liberally and without reproach, and it will be given to him" (James 1:5).

4. *Don't give the devil any place.* Faith repels the devil; fear empowers him. "Nor give place to the devil" (Eph. 4:27).

Therefore submit to God. Resist the devil and he will flee from you.

—JAMES 4:7

I say to you, have faith (keep your focus on Christ and His cross), stand firm (on the Word of God—the Word works when you work the Word in you), ask for wisdom (ask God for direction and proclamation over your life and challenges that come your way), and don't give the enemy any room to work in your life (when in doubt, don't; if you haven't heard from God, keep asking and proclaim the life of God and His Word over the situation until God gives you clarity).

If a double-minded man can expect nothing from God, according to James 1:7, then if you are focused on Jesus and His will, you trust His Word to do what it says it will do in your life, you add to your life daily faith, ever-increasing faith, then what do you think you can expect from God? He who has faith and does not doubt can expect everything God has promised to come to pass.

WHEN LIFE DEALS US THE UNEXPECTED, FOLLOW THE STILL VOICE OF GOD!

> Surely the Lord God does nothing, Unless He reveals His secret to His servants the prophets.
>
> —Amos 3:7

Have you ever heard someone say, "I wasn't expecting this; I never saw it coming"? Actually, most likely, when we look back and survey our lives, we will see warning signs all over. Life deals us unexpected turns, but were they really unexpected?

As children of God, He warns us. Unfortunately, we do not listen for His still small voice. Our children often do not listen to us as parents; even though they hear a parent talking, it goes in one ear and out the other. We as Christians are no different in our daily walk with God. Have you ever heard a parent say to a child, "Did you not hear me when I was speaking to you?" Most of the time the child says yes, with a questioned look wondering all the while what did they say?

We as adults can learn from children; we too do the same thing. We go to God in prayer, and when He starts to speak we get up, go on our way, only to find later we need God's help. He already told us what was going to happen, and what we would need to do, yet we did not truly hear it because we were doing our thing. Life deals unexpected circumstances. If we have listened in our prayer time not only will we know what to do, but we can also know what is coming our way. The old saying is, "to be forewarned is to be forearmed." God wants to speak into our lives so we may not be dealt the unexpected without having His love, power, and direction to bring us through those times victoriously. May we me to listen closer to Your voice so that each moment, our desire is to be in the center of Your will, Lord.

> And he said, Go forth, and stand upon the mount before the Lord. And, behold, the Lord passed by, and a great and strong wind rent the mountains, and brake in pieces the rocks before the Lord; but the Lord was not in the wind: and after the wind an earthquake; but the Lord was not in the earthquake: And after the earthquake a fire; but the Lord was not in the fire: and after the fire a still small voice.
>
> —1 Kings 19:11–12, kjv

It often takes the unexpected to get us to ask God to hear His voice. God desires to speak to each one of His children on a daily basis, to direct our lives to be fruitful and powerful for His glory. We too are a lot like Elijah; we look for God in all the big things of life, when all the while He was in a still small voice. Seek God before the unexpected comes, and you will find that your will is in the center of His, no matter what you may face, expected or unexpected, you will hear His voice.

~ 56 ~

ADVERSITY: GOD'S TOOL TO REFINE US!

> But as for you, you meant evil against me; *but* God meant it for good, in order to bring it about as *it is* this day, to save many people alive.
> —GENESIS 50:20, NKJV

HAVE YOU BEEN TRANSFORMED THROUGH THE FLAMES OF ADVERSITY?

ONE OF THE names for Satan is *adversary*. What is his number one job? Deceive the believer by bringing adversity into our lives. Adversity will do one of two things to us: it will leave us beaten down, settling for less, or it will spur us on to go into the deeper things of God. Where are you today? Have you let adversity, or the adversary, win? Or are you going to make up your mind to have the mind of Christ and be all He created you to be?

> I advise you to buy from Me gold refined by fire, that you may become rich, and white garments, that you may clothe yourself, and that the shame of your nakedness may not be revealed; and eye salve to anoint your eyes, that you may see.
> —REVELATION 3:18, NASU

Adversity can block your sight and wreck your emotions if you allow it to!
—SHEILA ZELLERS

Adversity—what is it? *Webster's* puts it this way:

1. A state or condition contrary to one of well-being.

2. An instance of adversity; misfortune.

Have You Been Going Through the Refiner's Fire or Burn Out?

Satan desires to burn out, and then burn up God's children. When you decide to go with God no matter what, then you will see Satan for who he is—a liar and a loser—and you will welcome the Refiner's Fire. For as you go into the presence of God and He disposes of the past, pain, and unworthiness, you will come out shining of His presence and glory.

> Refiner: verb—1: to free (as metal, sugar, or oil) from impurities or unwanted material; to free from moral imperfection: ELEVATE; to lift up; to rise in the rank or status: EXALT

If you are among those who know the fire of affliction and chose to endure the refining process allowed by God, then the sound of the word *adversity* does not resonate fear in your spirit. For if you know God is carrying you through the fire of refining, then you will know He will be your strength.

If you have been crying out for more of Him, be sure you will have to go through the Refiner's Fire to have Him! For it is through the Refiner's Fire your faith and you will become like Him. God desires a pure heart to serve Him in spirit and in truth.

> But the hour cometh, and now is, when the true worshippers shall worship the Father in spirit and in truth: for the Father seeketh such to worship him.
> —JOHN 4:23, KJV

For us to be more like Jesus, we must deny self, die to the carnal nature, and live unto Christ. To become more like Christ, we must be willing to go into the Refiner's Fire.

Why the fires? Why such difficulty? What is left in the wake of the purging of the flesh? It is a daily reminder that it is not about us but about Him. We must go through every dimension of purging and allow the transformed "man/woman" to emerge as a person who has conquered. The presence of God through the Refiner's fire will allow faith in God to increase.

There is a strength that arises, when "trust" in the unseen realm of the spirit is challenging and beckoning us to move ahead out of the comfort zone and spirit of complacency.

> (As it is written, *"I have made you a father of many nations"*) in the presence of Him whom he believed—God, who gives life to the dead and calls those things which do not exist as though they did.
> —ROMANS 4:17

Being truly sold out to God is not a job for wimps. In fact, it takes a great step of faith. It will break you down to nothing in order for Him to make something beautiful in and out of your life.

Remember, all adversity does not come from Satan, even though evil is the root. We can make adversity in our own lives by not allowing God to correct our hearts, by disobedience to God's commands, or out of selfish desires or ambitions.

Many have become radically familiar with the moves of God in this hour. All who are called to high levels of spiritual revelation, financial trust, and business, in a day and time where everything seems to be going downhill, believe we will prosper and bless others and operate in our God-given spiritual authority. We must welcome the Refining Fire of God in our lives. God is no respecter of persons. He is calling us all to the *higher heights and deeper depths in Him*.

> Deep calls unto deep at the noise of your waterfalls; All Your waves and billows have gone over me.
> —PSALM 42:7

For we know this is where His true gold is found, gold that will not rust or melt away, but will endure for all eternity. We go into the Fire of Refining to help ourselves then in turn help others.

> But who can endure the day of His coming? And who can stand when He appears? For He *is* like a refiner's fire and like launderer's soap. He will sit as a refiner and a purifier of silver; He will purify the sons of Levi, and purge them as gold and silver, that they may offer to the LORD an offering in righteousness.
> —MALACHI 3:2–3

This word *refine* literally means "to burn or be tried." Each trial we go through will teach us what we need to know to be more like God and to serve others.

In Revelation 3:18, we are told to buy gold from God that we may be truly wealthy or rich in Him. That we may see with His eyes. Buy gold from the gold maker *not* the imitator, Satan. Don't let your past failures and sins hold you captive to never succeed.

> As far as the east is from the west, so far has He removed our transgressions from us.
>
> —PSALM 103:12

See with God's eyes what He called you and appointed you to be and do. Satan gives you a dismal picture, but God gives you life and shows you what He sees you becoming. When you have His gold and when you have gone through the fire with the intent of being changed, God will show and direct you to His path.

57

HIDDEN ROOTS PRODUCE BAD FRUIT IN THE HEART!

Keep your heart with all diligence, for out of it *spring* the issues of life.

—Proverbs 4:23

THERE ARE MANY reasons why someone hides things: to keep a secret, to keep a thing secure, to pretend it did not happen, to save for later, or to keep the truth from coming out! Hidden things of the heart can be great or they can produce torment. When the angel appeared to the mother of our Lord, Mary, she was told she was chosen to be the one to give birth to the Christ Child, the Messiah. The Word of God says she hid these things in her heart. Did she hide them because she was afraid, or did she hide them because they were too great? Maybe she thought no one would believe her even if she did reveal them to another.

The hidden things of the heart can be which bring pain in your memories and mind. When you think about them, a fear of man comes up and you become afraid of being found out or exposed. They can be things of the past or future which can bring pain in either your memories or your mind. They can be things you have done. or that have been done to you. You can carry the agony of "what ifs" over the course of your life, which have kept you imprisoned to your past. These kind of hidden things have a bad root from the start. They were not birthed out of the heart of God, but out of the fear of man. We do not serve a God of exposure, but of purpose and plan for His glory in every area of our lives.

> The fear of the Lord *is* clean, enduring forever; the judgments of the Lord *are* true *and* righteous altogether. More to be desired *are they* then gold, Yea, than much fine gold;

sweeter also than honey and the honeycomb. Moreover by them Your servant is warned, *and* in keeping them *there is* great reward.

—PSALM 19:9–11

If we are not careful with the pains of yesterday, they will grow and become stumbling stones of failure in our spiritual lives. God desires to bring all things to light which are hidden due to secret sins, rejection, persecutions, abandonment, or the feeling of unworthiness. God desires to expose your darkness to His glorious light that you may be healed to be all He called and created you to be!

How to Detect if There Are Hidden Things in the Heart

Hidden things of the heart form over time.

Hidden things form by many things coming together to create a matter of the heart. Hidden things did not get there overnight; it takes time, pain to pain, hurt to hurt, rejection to rejection. When not dealt with, they will begin to fester, then grow to form hidden hurts.

You can cover them for a while, but when you least expect it, your emotions will play tricks on you to expose what is really in your heart. This is how Satan operates. He likes you to think you are fine, then sudden impact happens; this is where he tries to steal, kill, and destroy. Things we chose to cover up rather than expose to the light of God come back to haunt us.

> Therefore do not fear them. For there is nothing covered that will not be revealed, and hidden that will not be known.
>
> —MATTHEW 10:26, NKJV

Hidden things grow over a span of time when wrongly covered.

Just because the pain of something seems to stop or go away, if we have not dealt with it, it will show up again. Time has a way of telling the truth about what is in our heart; good or bad, right or wrong, painful or glad, it all shows forth in time. If we cover the pain of an event, it will show up if not dealt with. God is honest; He asks us as His children to be open and honest with Him that He may heal the brokenness within our hearts.

No one else may know this is in our hearts, but you and I know when pain is growing within us. It seems we become very defensive to keep anyone from knowing how wounded we may really be. This produces fear and a war between us and God.

> For nothing is secret that will not be revealed, nor *anything* hidden that will not be known and come to light.
> —LUKE 8:17

Hidden things of the heart will suffocate the life out of you.
Self and Satan want you to think and even believe these hidden things are not there! Then all of a sudden, they come up to make you feel like everything is going wrong. However, have you looked to see where the root of the feeling is? Could it be there is an unresolved issue in your heart?

You have been wounded by a brother or sister in the faith, in your family, or at work, and the truth is, you will hide it and then you will replay it, then you will baby it, then you will deny it to the point that you begin to lie to yourself, pretending it never really happened, the whole time giving fuel to Satan to use it to stop the will of God in your life. Out of your heart flow the issues of life.

> Keep vigilant watch over your heart; *that's* where life starts. The worst lie one can tell is to one's self! This is Satan's most valuable tool in the believer's life: to get him or her to lie to one's self.
> —PROVERBS 4:23, THE MESSAGE

Hidden things will keep you from having an honest heart.
The worst heart to lie to is your own. Christians, even I—yes, me—lie to ourselves. It is hard to admit, but so true. Unfortunately, when your back is against the wall and you think you are going to be exposed, you will lie! Do you want to? Hopefully not, but with God's love and strength, when the Lord reveals an issue in your heart, it shows that He decided that you are ready to face the hidden thing through His wisdom and love. God will never reveal a secret

sin, fault, or failure if He is not willing to heal you from the inside out. He does not expose and then leave one hurting with no remedy to be healed, whole, and redeemed.

Hidden things of our heart will be healed!

King David had sinned with Bathsheba; he had misused his authority as king. In Psalm 19:12–13, he asks God to cleanse him from his secret faults and his presumptuous sins. These hidden things can be sins we committed or the pain of sins committed against us that we have held on to.

We have to be willing to welcome and accept the convicting power of the Holy Spirit. God will find a way to let you know you need a healing in your heart. Forgiveness is the greatest power a believer has, first to us and then to others. The Word of God says it is God's goodness that leads men to repentance; through His Spirit and love He ministers to believers to work on the issues of our hearts. Hidden roots produce bad fruit, but God's love heals to bring life, light, and love to allow God to take up the old and plant anew in you His life, for His glory.

~ 58 ~

DO YOU NEED A SPIRITUAL TUNE-UP?

Just as a vehicle needs maintenance, so does each Christian.

I F YOU ARE a human being, you will encounter people on a daily basis that will drain your energy, clog your pipes, or stuff up your heart with cares of this life! Maybe you are in need of a spiritual tune-up.

Have you ever asked yourself the question, "God, where are you in all of this?" or "Where did my power in Jesus go?" If we are not renewing our minds in Christ, we will lose our power in Him! Things of life will weary us; if we do not cast our cares over and forgive the offenses that come our way, we will be powerless and not even know it! Releasing the pain of yesterday will recharge your spiritual life!

> Brethren, I do not count myself to have apprehended; but one thing *I do*, forgetting those things which are behind and reaching forward to those things which are ahead.
> —PHILIPPIANS 3:13

If you are an adult, you have either driven, owned, rented, or borrowed a car before. If you purchase a car, you are given an instruction manual regarding what to do with the car, especially during its warranty. Car maintenance and forgiveness have a lot in common. You see, having one's car oil changed is a lot like being cleansed from unforgiveness!

Do you want your power back? Do you want to operate in the anointing of God? Unforgiveness will clog the intake of your heart in the same way not having your oil changed will slow your car down and even clog up the air filter and eventually build up carbon which can damage the engine. Forgiveness is not approval or acceptance of what others have done. It's releasing your own heart to be forgiving so you and the other person can be free in Jesus!

Selahs from God

Reconciliation may not happen in forgiveness. If it can, that is great. If not, it doesn't always mean you have not forgiven. It may be best for the past to be the past and, like Paul and Barnabas, you are better to grow in God on separate journeys. Forcing relationships back together may not be the best thing. Unless God rebuilds the relationship, it is best not to rebuild at all!

Internal junk comes from emotional garbage you take in that corrupts the heart! Forgiveness should not be a duty to God, but a privilege as a believer. One could do it out of appreciation to God for His love toward you while you were still a sinner. But why not forgive because you were forgiven? While you were in sin, God did not hold your sin against you, so what gives you the right to hold sin against others?

You don't want to grieve the Spirit of God in your life, as well in the ones who have hurt you. True forgiveness forgives and then desires the ones who hurt you to prosper and grow in God. If you are a true Christian, you desire to have a spiritual tune-up, an oil change for God's glory, to have your heart pure and operating the way God formed it to, in the image of Jesus Christ.

Forgiveness is not saying I agree with the pain or sin someone has caused or done. It says, "I love God more than this pain, so I am choosing to let go of your sin to be free." In the process, those who hurt you will have an opportunity to be forgiven and free. Not forgiving does not clog others' hearts up; it only hurts yours.

Living in forgiveness is supernatural, and it becomes praise to God's glory. It becomes doable, which makes it durable! Unlike the maintenance on your car, you should not wait five months, or five thousand miles, whichever comes first. Forgiveness should be an instant obedience; instant forgiveness should become a lifestyle for the Christian, to God's glory!

Are you in need of a spiritual tune-up?

59

PRAYING WHAT'S ON GOD'S HEART

> Wherefore he is able also to save them to the uttermost that come unto God by him, seeing he ever liveth to make intercession for them.
>
> —HEBREWS 7:25, KJV

BORN-AGAIN HUMANS ARE the vessels God uses to make intercession through. It is not our power but God's Son ministering through us. When we go into prayer asking God what He desires for us to pray, only then can He operate His power through us to make and break powers of the devil *off our* lives and *others through Jesus.*

> Likewise the Spirit also helpeth our infirmities: for we know not what we should pray for as we ought: but the Spirit itself maketh intercession for us with groanings which cannot be uttered.
>
> —ROMANS 8:26, KJV

Every Christian is called to pray. Many will say they have a gift of intercession, but the truth is we all need to pray 1 Timothy 2:1–2. All Christians may not pray the same amount. Some are given a greater desire than others, but all are called to pray. You're an intercessor (every believer is called to pray), but you cannot do the intercession that He is doing for you. There is no physical way for you to do that. So, it is best that you let Him do His job, and you do yours, which is: 1) obey what He asks of you, 2) love the Lord your God with all your heart, and 3) love your neighbor as you love yourself.

> Who shall separate us from the love of Christ? shall tribulation, or distress, or persecution, or famine, or nakedness, or peril, or sword? As it is written [Remember, Jesus

spoke those words in the wilderness]: For thy sake we are killed all the daylong; we are accounted as sheep for the slaughter. Nay, in all these things [How many things? *All these things!*] we are more than conquerors through him that loved us. For I am persuaded, that neither death, nor life, nor angels, nor principalities, nor powers, nor things present, nor things to come, Nor height, nor depth, nor any other creature, shall be able to separate us from the love of God, which is in Christ Jesus our Lord.

—Romans 8:35–39

Look at the Scripture. It says "nor any other created thing." Ninety-nine percent of all the troubles that you have in your life are created things, created beings. They are all going to pass away. Why do you think the Lord inspired the writer to put in *all* created things?

For we wrestle not against flesh and blood, but against principalities, against powers, against the rulers of the darkness of this world, against spiritual wickedness in high places.

—Ephesians 6:12

Your prayer life will be more effective by interceding what Jesus is interceding at the throne.

There He is also able to save the uttermost those who come to God through Him, since He always lives to make intercession for them.

—Hebrews 7:25, NKJV

We can pray our wish list or we can pray the heart of Jesus, what God is instructing Him to pray today. Are you praying righteous fervent prayers? When you pray what Jesus is praying, then you are praying the Father's heart.

And the prayer of faith will save the sick, and the Lord will raise him up. And if he has committed sins, he will be forgiven. Confess your trespasses to one another, and pray for one another, that you may be healed. The effective, fervent prayer of a righteous man avails much.

—James 5:15–16, NKJV

Praying What's On God's Heart

God's not a Christmas list God. He's not a Bisquick fix God. He's not a drive-thru and call it homemade God. He's a true God, a just God, a righteous God, He's a holy God. And do you know what? Everything He is, *you are,* if you're willing to go with God. Are you willing to do it His way? God is not a have-it-your-way God; it is according to His Word in John 14:16, He is the way, the truth, and the life.

God's saying we need to conform to *His* Spirit, Word, and will.

To pray what *His* Son is praying around the throne, you'll need to break some old habits. Scientifically it is proven it takes about twenty-one days to build a habit but a lifetime to break it. That's why you have to be transformed by Romans 12:1 and 2. You have to renew the mind by the Word of God, transforming yourself to God's will.

When you choose to pray the Father's heart and desires, your prayer life is going to change.

> The steps of a good man are ordered by the Lord: and he delighteth in his way. Though he fall, he shall not be utterly cast down: for the Lord upholdeth him with his hand.
> —PSALM 37:23–24

The Lord will uphold you. When you pray it is vital that you ask Jesus, "What are you interceding about my life or in certain situations?" *What is the Father saying*?

Not long ago, I went into prayer and I was doing my thing. Just because I preach it, I still forget too! And all of a sudden, the Holy Spirit asked me, "Aren't you going to ask Me what concerns Me today?" Because I was going to go with my prayer list. So I asked, "Father God, what are you having Your Son intercede for today?" This is what He told me to pray for: "Bosnia. Pray for Bosnia." I had no idea *why Bosnia.*

I was stumped. I asked Him about it. He said, "That is a war-torn country. That is a country that missionaries are being martyred in. It's not being put on TV because it is an awful sight. This is horrid."

The next day, I was praying for the missionaries and the Holy Spirit said, "Call Dan Betzer." He's the pastor from Revival Time through the First Assembly of God, Fort Myers. I said, "Call Dan

Betzer? Why?" He said, "*Because Bosnia is in his heart and it concerns him.*"

I didn't obey. I didn't figure that little ol' me could get through to him, even though we are friends and we went to Israel with him. I got busy teaching that day. The next day I called, and Pastor Betzer had left for Israel. I asked the secretary for forgiveness, because I had not obeyed the Lord that day He told me to do this. Her words were, "Oh yes, honey, he'll call you when he gets back. Bosnia concerns him." Then she gave me a list of names of missionaries there to pray for. I prayed for them, but I know it wasn't God's perfect will because I was not obedient to His direction.

When you sow in prayer, *God's heart, God's concerns, then* God will take care of what's in your life. *Praying the Father's heart will redirect you to others and their needs.*

> Seek ye first the kingdom of God, and His righteousness, and all these things will be added unto you.
> —MATTHEW 6:33

He wants to change your life today. He wants to make your life different. Your life will only be different through the power of the Word and interceding according to the Word, getting your pathway directed by God Almighty, not by your wants, and not by *your desires.*

God desires His children to think and pray worldwide. God wants you to have His heart. *He wants your heart to be created in His image.* He desires His Word be the center of all you do in life and in prayer time.

Have you asked God today what is on His heart for you to pray about concerning the things in your life, in the world around you, in your family?

> Confess your trespasses to one another, and pray for one another, that you may be healed. The effective, fervent prayer of a righteous man avails much.
> —JAMES 5:16

~ 60 ~

DON'T ALLOW MAN TO DEFINE WHAT GOD DESIGNED

> Dear friends, now we are children of God, and what we will be has not yet been made known. But we know that when Christ appears, we shall be like him, for we shall see him as he is. All who have this hope in him purify themselves, just as he is pure.
>
> —1 John 3:2–3, niv

From the beginning of time God's design was for man to be like Him. He created man from the dust of the earth in His likeness, His image, His blue print. That design has not changed from the first man, Adam. God has not changed His mind on His heart toward you and me. God designed man to be His family. He wants each man, woman and child to be like Him, to love like Him and most of touch others on this earth like Him. God designed man for relationship with Him first, then others.

In our world today we are told how we are to look, feel, believe, react and if we don't fit into the perfect little mold then we have a pill for that! God did not call us to conform to this world or religion. He called each human who has trusted, relied upon and received Jesus Christ as their Savior to be transformed! Transformed by His Spirit into the person He designed, called and anointed us to be. He loves you and me just like we are, but He does not want us to stay there! He desires us to grow in Him, His love, and likeness. God's design for and me is to become more like Him each and every day.

To live by God's design we are going to have to know the word of God and His ways. What the world calls acceptable, the word of God calls compromise. When we as Christians start looking, acting and sounding like the world we deceive ourselves. Jesus came to give hope and a future in Him. God is not concerned about our happiness as much as he is our character; His design for us is to be more like Him.

Don't allow man to define what God has designed you to be for God's glory. He called you out of darkness into His wonderful Light. He desires for you to be like Him, then to share His love, light and hope with all you meet. When we allow our circumstances to rule who we are, we will never measure up to God or man, in other words we lose.

God never called us to be losers, compromising, defeated, down and out, woe is me, fearful people; He calls us to be righteous believers, victorious warriors, winners for His glory. Never allow your feelings to rule you, they will defeat you; look for God's design in everything you do and you will find He is there! And when He appears you will be like Him! Who's design are you living by, the worlds or the Word?

NOTES

IN THE MIDST OF YOUR BATTLE, REMEMBER HIS MERCY ENDURES FOREVER!

1. *TouchPoint Bible, New Living Translation* (Carol Stream, IL: Tyndale House Publishers, 1996).

GOD SETS YOUR WORTH; YOU ARE THE APPLE OF HIS EYE

1. *Holman Bible Dictionary*, s.v. "Apple of the eye," (Nashville: Broadman & Holman, 1991). All rights reserved. Used by permission of Broadman & Holman.

TRUST IS PRODUCED IN GOD'S PRESENCE

1. *The American Heritage Dictionary of the English Language*, 4th ed., s.v. "Delight."

ABOUT THE AUTHOR

REVEREND SHEILA ZELLERS is an anointed and powerful preacher, teacher, prophet and evangelist, Christian recording artist and composer. She is a native Floridian who makes her home in Naples, Florida, with her husband, Tim, her high school sweetheart, married since 1977. They have two adult children: Joy, married to Dustin, and A.J. to Natalie. They have been blessed with three grandchildren. She ministers through word and music at area retreats, conferences and churches across the nation and around the world. Sheila has also been the featured soloist at the National Conferences and Regional Retreats of Aglow International. She has a divine call on her life to minister the illuminating, liberating, healing touch of Jesus Christ to God's people through worshiping the Lord in the splendor of His holiness.

Sheila has served in Aglow International since 1987, and was president of Naples Day from 1987–1993. In the summer of 1993, she felt God gave her a new vision for pioneering a second Lighthouse in Naples Night Aglow that would meet the needs of working women. Because of this vision, a new evening Lighthouse was established where she served as president until 1998. Sheila served on the Southwest Florida Area Team of Aglow International from 1999–2007.

Sheila founded Motivated by Love Ministries in 2000, an evangelistic outreach ministry, which holds monthly outreach meetings in Naples to equip the body of Christ to be all God created them to be. Motivated by Love Ministries also supports missions in the USA, Africa, and Europe. Sheila has hosted her weekly radio program, MBL Radio Live, since 1995, and pioneered her MBL Live TV program in 2011. Her radio, TV, and monthly MBL Encounters can be viewed through her www.MotivatedbyLove.org website.

Having personally experienced sickness, defeat, and abuses of many kinds in her life, Sheila has witnessed the resurrection power of Jesus Christ in the restoration and renewal of her spirit, soul and body. God has given her revelation knowledge to bring others with

About the Author

emotional dysfunctions in their lives through deliverance and into freedom from bondage and wholeness in Him.

Sheila and Tim attended New Hope Ministries from 1987 until 2003. Sheila taught at New Hope School of Ministries, Naples, Florida from 2000–07, teaching "The Holy Spirit" class. She sang on the praise team, served in women's ministry, altar team, and choir. She has been a staff member of Parkway Life Church of God since 2008, where Tim and Sheila have attended since 2003. Sheila is an ordained minister with the Church of God of Cleveland, Tennessee.

She is invited to minister in word, preaching, and teaching, as well as in ministry of praise and worship and solos. She and her MBL Worship Team are asked to be guest worship leaders at churches, conferences, and retreats across the nation. Sheila and Tim own four businesses as well, and Sheila is also involved in local radio and TV broadcast advertising for nonprofit ministries and organizations.

As Sheila ministers in word and in song with true humility and reverence for the Lord Jesus Christ our King, experience the glory of His grace and the power of His Holy Spirit as God inhabits the praises of His people.

CONTACT THE AUTHOR

Reverend Sheila Zellers
Motivated by Love Ministries, Inc.
3485 Mercantile Ave.
Naples, FL 34104

239-325-2740

RevSheilaZ@MotivatedByLove.org
www.MotivatedByLove.org